Girl Gone London

Girl Gone London

An American's Guide to Surviving Life in the UK

Kalyn Franke

Girl Gone London by Kalyn Franke

www.girlgonelondon.com

© 2021 Kalyn Franke

kalyn@girlgonelondon.com

Cover by Guy Mannerings.

ISBN: 978-1-9162124-0-4

For Grammy, who I wish could have held this book in her hands.

Contents

Introduction

"You will never be completely at home again. Because part of your heart will always be elsewhere. That is the price you pay for the richness of loving and knowing people in more than one place."

When I first started my expat life in January of 2012, I had that quote carefully taped to the wall behind my desk in an attempt to inspire myself to fully embrace the "journey" of life abroad.

A few years later, I aggressively ripped the quote down in a rage of expat homesickness while I ranted about small English houses, the lack of sunshine, and the fact that I couldn't find a Target anywhere.

Now, almost ten years into my expat journey in the UK, I've discovered that the truth of expat life lies somewhere in between thought-provoking quotes printed on a picture of a cloud and the quotes that I say when in a fit of expat depression that I'd rather not replicate here for fear of ruining my image to people who somehow still think I'm "cool and collected."

Though maybe it's important that I address now, before I go too far, that there is nothing "cool and collected" about expat life in the UK. In fact, there is nothing "cool and collected" about the British, despite them portraying themselves that way, which is a cultural truth you learn after dealing with people "tutting" at you on the tube for so many years. Who knew a person could express such hatred for you without saying a word?

No, expat life is not "cool and collected," but it *is* fun, messy, dynamic, scary, exciting, intense, sad, happy and a bunch of other words that basically mean, "hold onto your emotions, this is about to be a bumpy ride."

For me, expat life started as an American student on a study abroad program in London in 2012. While I started off the semester appreciative of my "once in a lifetime experience," it soon became clear to me that this didn't need to be once in a lifetime at all. It dawned on me, one morning while walking over Waterloo Bridge at 8:30am, that this hectically beautiful scene could be my life. I was fascinated by the fast pace of London and enchanted by the slow country lanes in villages across the UK. I was taken in by the accents, the fact that an entire nation could somehow feel prestigious, and a world that seemed to value quiet over noise.

After graduating from the University of Pittsburgh, I went on to do my Master's degree in London, then eventually met my now-husband, Guy (I was sold on him from the moment I heard he was an extra in the *Harry Potter* movies, what can I say?). I entered the UK workforce, we got engaged, we bought a house, we got married, and now I'm here, living the American expat life in southeast England while trying to figure out how to watch my American television shows without needing to log in to eight different sketchy programs or download a ton of viruses to my laptop.

While writing this book and dreaming up all the ways I could talk about my expat story, however, I struggled with what, exactly, I should share.

So just so that we're on the same page, I want you to know that this book isn't going to help you fill in your taxes or secure your next visa. Not only does best practice on this change constantly (I would highly recommend looking online for the answers or speaking to a qualified solicitor – by the way, can we talk about how it's so weird that solicitor means lawyer in the UK?), but that stuff is pretty boring.

What I do want to do is make sure you know that you aren't alone. Whether you're thinking of moving to the UK, in the process of doing so, or maybe you've been here for decades, I'm going to share my stories and experiences so you can finally confirm, without an English winter shadow of a doubt, that that weird thing you thought or that awkward moment you had wasn't just you.

I also want to get clear on things I wish somebody had told me before I moved here. Practical things, of course, but also things like, "Girl! You're not weird! Brits definitely do hang around after dinner in a restaurant for like 10 million hours and it's just the way it is. Sit your butt down."

See, when I first moved to the UK, I had no idea what was in store for me. My knowledge of British culture and the experience of being an American in the UK amounted to a lifelong desire to be Hermione Granger and stories told by my British hairdresser.

I had no idea how strong I could be and how much living in the UK would push me past any semblance of comfort zone I could have possibly created for myself. I couldn't have anticipated the tiny triggers that would make me break down in a supermarket, the capacity I had to adapt to new situations, or just how much I would end up liking Brussel sprouts.

This book is for anyone who needs a little (or a lot) of guidance when it comes to life in the UK as an American. From doubting your decision to move abroad to delighting in the joys of bank holidays to being irrationally homesick because you can't find Cinnamon Toast Crunch, you are not alone, and I want to tell you the things I've learned along the way.

And mostly, I want you to know that everything was, is, and will be okay. And not just okay, but sometimes wonderful in a way that you'll only ever know if you have or have had the *courage to go*.

Now, spoiler alert: it is physically impossible to write a book that covers every single question about expat life. Trust me, I've tried. No matter how much I write, there are always more things I want to add and if I let it go on forever, you wouldn't have been able to get your hands on this book right now.

So while you are about to be delighted with pages and pages and pages and pages of information, there is still a chance that you'll want to know even more. In fact, you definitely will.

To make sure that you have a space to ask all of those weird questions you think no one else has (they do) or you already live in the UK and want to commiserate about the lack of Smartfood White Cheddar popcorn, please get in touch at kalyn@girlgonelondon.com or head to GirlGoneLondon.com where you can navigate to the "Contact Me" page.

I would love to hear from you and connect you up with the online group so you can keep the conversation going!

Okay, buckle up. It's time to get in the British spirit and grab a cup of tea and go say "sorry" to a few people for no reason before jumping in to the book with all of your American enthusiasm!

Some Things are Out of Your Control
The Visa Headaches

I think it's appropriate to start this book with the thing that starts most of our journeys as expats in the UK: visa talk. Before we even learn what the heck Morrison's is or why everybody asks for a "plaster" instead of a "Band Aid," we have to engage in the expat ritual of discussing, fretting over, and generally having nightmares about our visas.

Even thinking about writing about my visa experiences makes me want to just curl up in a ball and wipe my tears with UKVI application forms. There is nothing more anxiety inducing than waiting for your visa approval, nothing more soul-destroying, and nothing more crazy-making.

I have made six visa applications since this whole expat adventure started for me: three Tier 4 visas (when they existed), one Tier 5 visa, one Unmarried Partner visa, and one renewal of that Partner visa.

The first two Tier 4 student visas were for semester study abroad programs through my American University (the University of Pittsburgh for any Pitt Panthers out there).

Wait – hold up one second. Did you catch that? I just wrote "university" instead of "college" like the wannabe British person I am. I went back to change it to "college," but I'm going to leave it in because it speaks an important truth about how many of us expats find ourselves subconsciously reverting to British phrases and words and what this means for our feelings (and confusion) about home and who we are.

But I'll get into that later – back to the regularly scheduled programming.

Anyway, the first two student visas were for study abroad semesters, then I had a short term student visa, which I didn't need to apply for in advance, for my third study abroad semester. By the time my undergraduate career was finished, I studied abroad through Pitt three semesters in total, thanks to lots of AP classes and a Communications major that allowed me the ability to not go to class from anywhere in the world.

My Tier 5 visa was a Work Experience visa through the BUNAC program, who basically agree to sponsor your short term work visa for about $800 if you find your own internship in the UK, or you can pay extortionate amounts for other companies to find you an internship

While on the Tier 5 visa, I interned for a company that sent food box subscriptions to your door. My job mostly consisted of listening to elderly women yell at me for sending them too many tomatoes, even though I had not actually had a role in the aforementioned tomato tragedy, and also I couldn't really understand most of the people on the phone because I was still getting used to British accents in a work context.

After my Tier 5 visa expired, I applied for my third Tier 4 visa application which was for my Master's degree in Public Relations at the University of Westminster. To be honest, I only applied for this degree because I was looking for legal ways to stay in the country, but I got a Master's degree out of it and didn't have to spend any more time talking about tomatoes, so it was a good decision overall.

Once I had graduated and was on the tail end of my final Tier 4 visa, I was able to switch onto an unmarried partner visa with my then-boyfriend.

If you're not familiar with the unmarried partner visa, it requires that you can prove you lived with your significant other in "a relationship akin to marriage" (so no roommate set ups) for at least two years, along with proving that you meet the same financial requirements as the married partner visa and have shared financial responsibilities.

As luck would have it, I didn't know about this particular visa route until the final months of my Tier 4 visa, and on the last day of my Tier 4 visa, we would have lived together for exactly two years.

This was one of those serendipitous expat moments that worked out for us – we didn't have to get married until we were actually ready to, and the day we said our "I Dos" in front of everyone was truly the day we were legally married.

If you are someone who has had to get married a bit earlier than you would have liked in a relationship in order to make sure that you and your partner could continue living together or could start to do so, I just want to let you know that there is no judgement here. I know how hard it was for so many of my friends who had to make the choice between "getting the paperwork," as it were, and marrying when they were ready and not the government.

But as with many things in expat life, we can only do the best with the rules we're given and the constraints we have. Sometimes the choices are hard, and we don't always look back on them fondly, but they're all part of our figurative journey, and that means something.

My latest visa application was simply a renewal of my partner visa, though this time filed under the "married" category.

Of course, spoiler alert: all of my visa applications have come back successful, but WOW, have I lost years of my life to sitting at the window, willing the postman to turn the corner and deliver my future.

The first few times I made visa applications under the student route, I had no real appreciation for the actual stress that could be involved. I mean, sure, I complained that I had to pay like a $400 fee (cute baby Kalyn, thinking $400 is a lot to pay to the Home Office). I probably complained that the paperwork wasn't entirely straightforward and I had to do crazy things like, *gasp*, take a photocopy of every page of my passport.

But when I made my visa application to switch from my student visa (a non-settlement visa) to my unmarried partner visa (to start on the settlement route), my mental stability quickly came tumbling down.

The Application Process

As I mentioned in the introduction, I'm not going to get into the nitty gritty of what you need to do in your visa application to pass with flying colors. For one thing, this seems to change constantly and one time I had literally filled out an entire application on paper only to discover they had updated the form about one day before I was going to submit it so I had to do it all again.

Also, it's illegal to give immigration advice in the UK if you're not a qualified immigration lawyer, which, thank goodness I'm not because I have better things to do with my time.

However, I have managed to divided the visa application process up into six mental stages, which I feel is far more useful in helping you feel slightly normal than telling you to make sure you don't forget to actually sign your name on your application (okay, well, there you go, one tip for you – don't leave out your John Hancock because you get so lost in the other requirements!)

Stage 1: Excitement

This is the "anything is possible if you just believe" stage.

Visa extension?

NO PROBLEM. I can't wait to continue my life in the UK!

What a joy that will be. Gosh, I love life. Look at all these blank pages to fill out proving my dedication to being a productive citizen of the UK.

What an ABSOLUTE TREAT this will be. Like meeting the Queen herself.

Stage 2: Fear

Wait, but what if they find a reason to make me leave?

Everything I've worked for so hard here will be gone in the blink of an eye.

OH MY GOD, I can't do this. This is too much pressure.

I don't want to look at this. Just let me cry in this corner, please.

Don't touch me.

Stage 3: Compulsive Organization

Okay, I've got six different sections with 13 documents each and an excel sheet for every entry.

Look at these color-coded clips, this will make it so much easier to read my application.

This is actually a thing of beauty.

TABLE OF CONTENTS FOR EVERYONE.

Stage 4: Panic

ARE YOU ACTUALLY KIDDING ME, MY VISA RENEWAL IS DUE IN 3 DAYS AND I HAVE NOTHING PREPARED.

DO NOT TRY TO TALK TO ME ABOUT THINGS OTHER THAN VISA DOCUMENTS OR I WILL BITE YOUR HEAD OFF.

OH MY GOD. OH MY GOD.

I AM HYPERVENTILATING. NOTHING IS GOING TO BE OKAY.

I QUIT. I'M MOVING BACK TO AMERICA.

Stage 5: Acceptance

Deep breath. I've done it. Goodbye, visa application.

Enjoy your journey through the internet and into the hands of a hopefully good-natured Entry Clearance Officer.

There is nothing I can do about it now.

I'm just going to relax, enjoy my life in the UK, and know that no matter what comes my way, everything will be just fine in the end.

Stage 6: Panic Some More

BUT WHAT IF IT'S NOT?!

WHAT IF THE IMMIGRATION OFFICER DOESN'T LIKE HOW I SPELL "SARAH" BECAUSE HIS DAUGHTER HAS IT WITHOUT THE "H" AND HE THINKS THAT'S THE ONLY WAY TO SPELL IT, AND THEN HE DENIES ME BECAUSE MY NAME IS STUPID AND,

OH MY GOD, WHAT IS HAPPENING?!

The Waiting Process

After you have successfully made it through the application process, which is a feat in and of itself, you're then thrust into the very uncomfortable waiting process.

Waiting for a visa rejection or approval is the absolute worst kind of waiting, because not only does it seem like your life hangs in the balance of the Home Office's wonky scales, but, if you don't use the priority service, there is no guaranteed date when it will come back.

Sure, there are "guidelines" as to approximately how long the Home Office is taking for your particular type of visa at that time, but it's just that – a guideline.

What I used to do is stalk internet forums where other poor souls listed out their timelines and frantically checked back to see when they received their visa so I could then equate it to my own timeline and try to predict when mine would come back.

Sometimes this worked, mostly it just made me crazy.

I remember when I was waiting for my unmarried partner visa to come back, we had a bay window at the time that opened out to the front of the apartment where I could see if the mailman was coming up the street.

I kid you not, I waited at that window for hours on end when it got close to the date I expected the answer in the mail – I sat like a dog, wagging its tail with abject fear and little self-awareness, while I waited for him to arrive.

And every day, as I watched him get out and go to the main reception building, I would try my best to study what was in his hands to see if there was anything that would have given me a glimmer of hope it contained a letter from the Home Office.

I'm not sure what I was expecting, really, because there was no way I could tell, but it helped me retain a slight semblance of control.

As soon as he had peeled out of the parking lot, I would RUN up to the reception building and burst through the door, looking expectedly at the receptionist who was still very much in the process of sorting the mail and could have really done without me interrupting her.

But interrupt her I did, because I have no chill, and every time she would look through and see if she received anything for me.

Finally, on a random Tuesday, she actually had received something for me, and it looked suspiciously like a letter from the Home Office. I grabbed it as fast as I could and ran back down the hill to my apartment with it clutched in my hands that were now sweating profusely.

Once I stepped inside, the true turmoil began.

The "Having No Control of Your Life" Process

As I stood in my bedroom, alone in the apartment, death gripping my letter from the Home Office, I couldn't bring myself to open it.

See, up until that point, everything was in my control. I was the one who filled out the application, I was the one who saved mail for the past two years to help confirm that I was living with my boyfriend full time, I was the one who had dutifully submitted copies of everything they asked for and I was the one who went to the post office and sent it on its merry way (now it's online!)

Except, in that moment, I had no control whatsoever. The answer in that letter would define my fate, or at least, that's how I felt at the time.

If I didn't open it, then surely I could just continue on blissfully in control. If I didn't open it, then I wouldn't have to see if it was an answer I didn't want. If I didn't open it, then my life would still be mine.

Even if you have already received countless visas back successfully and have no reason to think that the Home Office could deny you, there is still this uncomfortable, emotional, sinking feeling that comes with realizing that someone who is not you can decide whether you continue or begin to live in the country you have so desperately hoped to live in.

Further along in my expat journey, I have come to recognize this feeling as one that has helped me build up much resentment over the years – until you get citizenship, an expat's life in the UK is not their own. It is the one approved by the government. How much you can work, whether or not you can study, if you can start your own company, how soon you need to marry, how much you need to make – these decisions that many people take for granted are instead made for you with little input on your part, besides what basically amounts to begging.

I'll touch more on this resentment and how to cope with these expat feelings later on (trust me, it's not some of the ways I've tried), but for now, I want to end this section by defining and describing the basic options for moving to the UK.

Can you Google this? Absolutely you can. You can also Google "how do I do calculus," but sometimes you just need someone to explain it to you in words that are easier to understand than a calculus textbook or the Home Office guidance notes, which just so happen to be similar in how confusing they are and also how much they make you question how they arrived at the answer they did.

I also want you to know about these options now, so that you can plan more accurately for your future in the UK rather than how I did it, which was less dedicated planning and more accidental stumbling while being like, "No worries, British boyfriend, I'm American and with that comes a treasure trove of unbelievable optimism in the face of reality – it will be fine!"

Before I dig into these visa types, know that if you have no need for this, you should skip to the next section now unless you feel your life will be greater enriched by talk of visas (hey, who am I to say it won't?). If you do have a need for this, please note that this is not immigration advice and simply a description of some of the visas available and the basic requirements.

Did you note that? Not. Immigration. Advice.

And if you do need immigration advice, as much as I would so love to help, you wouldn't contact me about it unless you've already forgotten, in the span of about three paragraphs, my story about how I came to qualify for my settlement visa – accidental stumbling, remember?!?

Fiancé Visa

If you're coming to the UK to marry your partner within the six months after you arrive, you can apply for the fiancé visa. You must switch onto a married partner visa within six months in order to stay in the UK, however, so this is really only a temporary solution for someone who just wants to be in the country for wedding planning and to start their life together sooner.

Partner Visa (Unmarried)

Have you lived together with your partner for at least two years in a "relationship akin to marriage?" I mean, ask your boyfriend/girlfriend, HEY,

DUDE, is this a relationship akin to marriage?

If it is, it basically means that you share financial responsibilities like rent or a mortgage, probably bills, and perhaps you have a shared bank account.

You can get this visa if you have lived together for two years in any country, as long as you have documentation of your shared address and other things to back up the fact that you lived together in a relationship. There is also a financial requirement where the person who is the "sponsor" has to be making at least a certain amount, or your income can count towards it if you are currently living in the UK while applying for the visa.

The partner visa lasts for two and a half years, and then you have to renew for another two and a half years before you can get Indefinite Leave to Remain.

Partner Visa (Married)

The married partner visa is almost exactly the same as the unmarried partner visa, except that you need to show your marriage certificate and you don't have to have been living in the same place for the past two years the first time you get it. When you go to renew, obviously they will want to see that you've been, you know, married and living together, but if you haven't for various reasons, there is room to explain that.

This also has the same financial requirement, and lasts for two and a half years (then renewed for two and a half more years) before you can get Indefinite Leave to Remain.

Student Visa

A student visa is what it sounds like, but is not a route to "settlement," or "Indefinite Leave to Remain." You can only get this visa if you are attending a qualified institution, and they will give you further instructions to apply.

You can be on multiple student visas throughout the years – some short term, for maybe a short study abroad program, or longer ones, say, three years if you're doing your entire degree in the UK.

You can switch from a student visa to say, a partner visa or a Skilled worker visa, but there are rules and regulations surrounding this to look into if you're interested.

Temporary Worker Visa

The only way that most Americans can get the Temporary Worker visa is through a program that is sponsoring them using this "work experience" visa, like BUNAC. BUNAC is an organization that will sponsor your work experience/internship visa. You can find your own internship and pay less money, or they can find one for you for a hefty fee.

You cannot extend the temporary worker visa into other visas, so this is a pretty dead end route for an expat who wants to stay long term.

Innovator Visa or Start-up Visa

These visas are for those of you who a) somehow have lots of money in investment funds ready to start a company or b) can find an institution to sponsor you to start up your own company.

If you've got grand ideas, lots of connections, and loads of cash, check these out. These aren't one of the more common ways for Americans to become expats in the UK, but if this sounds like you, look it up!

Skilled Worker Visa

A skilled worker visa is the holy grail of visas among Americans who don't have relationship ties to the UK. This is, in essence, a work visa where the company you work for will "sponsor you" and confirm to the government that they need to employee you.

This can be a hard one to get, especially if you are entry level as UK companies won't go the extra mile to sponsor you when they could just get someone from the UK, but there are plenty of Americans on this type of visa.

The financial requirements with this visa come with a salary requirement that you need to meet in order for your job to qualify for a skilled worker visa position.

Intra-Company Visa

Sometimes, companies have locations in multiple countries, and send staff from one country to the other through the Intra-company visa. The key to this visa is that you are a "transfer," so you already had the job in the US before you then got the transfer position in the UK.

Other Visa Categories

There are plenty of other visa categories to investigate if you have a special situation, like if you spent a lot of your childhood in the UK, if you have some type of ancestry situation with the UK, or if you are a famous entertainer like Ariana Grande. And if Ariana Grande is reading this book, then we've got other questions besides what visa you need to get.

Indefinite Leave to Remain

Indefinite Leave to Remain is what many expats strive to get, as this is a "settlement" visa that allows you to live in the UK without continually reapplying for new visas (hence the "indefinite.") You will want to check that your current visa category is able to qualify you for Indefinite Leave to Remain, as time as a student, for example, doesn't count towards the years you must live in the UK in order to secure Indefinite Leave to Remain.

For many American expats, this is a now a five-year route and most of us end up qualifying due to either partner or work visas. The requirements are different for both, in the sense that obviously qualifying with a partner visa is going to come along with certain criteria to ensure you are still in that relationship, and qualifying with a work visa entails ensuring your company still needs you and you still make the necessary salary. There are other ways to obtain this, too, so do your research when the time comes.

UK Citizenship

Citizenship is the final frontier for American expats, as we are allowed to hold dual UK and US citizenships. Once you qualify for and receive UK citizenship, you will then qualify for a UK passport and the days of visas are completely and truly over.

It is costly, in the thousands of pounds, but worth getting for peace of mind. There are additional requirements to qualify for citizenship which include a "Life in the UK" test about UK culture, history, and more, as well as character references and in-depth checks on your UK immigration history.

As with anything visa related, there are so many rules, regulations, and ever-changing stipulations that make applying for and receiving a visa or citizenship to the UK a long journey filled with lots of hair pulling for many of us.

But don't worry too much – much like giving birth (allegedly), you'll eventually forget the exact pain you were in at the time and it will be filled with happy memories of getting the acceptance through the mail. You'll soon learn to be stressed about other things, like whether your visa picks its clothes up off the floor even though you told them to put it in the hamper like 86 times.

Or something like that.

UK Basics
What You Need to Know to Not Embarrass Yourself

When I was a study abroad student, one of our professors gave us a blank map and asked us to label the countries in the UK. After about five minutes of us all randomly placing cities, borders and rivers onto a map, it soon became clear that we had come all the way to the UK without knowing much at all. I'm pretty sure I thought Wales was in Ireland and tried to place Northern Ireland in Britain, and if you had tried to explain to me what any of that meant, I would probably have looked at you with a blank face.

It doesn't help that many Americans have a very limited idea of what is even across the Atlantic on the "other side of the pond," as it were, and to this day I think most people still think that London is England and England is the same thing as the United Kingdom. Then again, if you ask Brits to label the states on a USA map, I think you'd get much of the same.

One of the best parts of being an expat in the UK is that you're going to embarrass yourself over and over again, and you're going to have to learn to laugh at yourself because that's the proper British way to get over it.

In an effort to spare you some of the most embarrassing American blunders, however, I've put together a little bit of a cheat sheet when it comes to the basics of the UK that you should really try and commit to memory. Or at least store this book in your bag so you can run into the bathroom and take a peek at it whenever the need arises.

UK Geography

Looking at the Big Picture

The most confusing thing for Americans is figuring out the difference between England, Great Britain, the United Kingdom, Wales, Scotland, and Northern Ireland (some of you are probably like, 'there's a Northern Ireland?!').

So let's get this straight. Think of the two islands that are next to each other when we think of "across the pond."

The one on the left, the smaller one, is made up of Ireland and Northern Ireland.

The one on the right is made up of Scotland, Wales, and England. Scotland is at the top, England is basically the big middle chunk, and Wales is NOT the bottom most bit that sticks out, but the bit above that that sticks out to the left.

Now, both of these islands together are called the British Isles.

The United Kingdom, however, is made up of Northern Ireland, Scotland, England, and Wales.

And Great Britain actually refers to just the island on the right and the countries that make it up – Scotland, England, Wales (and some other smaller islands).

Ireland is not a part of the United Kingdom or Great Britain.

Try to memorize these distinctions so you're not referring to the United Kingdom when you mean Great Britain or England when you mean the United Kingdom or any other combination you can think of.

Zooming In

When you take a closer look at the countries that make up the United Kingdom and what's involved, you're going to start discovering "counties." Like counties in the US, these are smaller subsets of the country that share geographical boundaries.

You'll soon learn the name of your county and any shorthand for it, and you'll also have the joy of trying to pronounce things like "Gloucestershire." There are a lot of "-shires" to figure out, and soon you'll feel like a character out of Robin Hood as you try to learn the lay of the land.

Weather

There are a few stereotypes about the UK that are incredibly true, and one of those is how "damp" it is. Now, it doesn't necessarily have the highest number of rainy days – some cities in America like Seattle are much rainier. But the climate, known as temperate maritime, means that it is, overall, a drizzly country. This is wonderful for the greenery that surrounds the countryside, and pretty terrible for people who are used to sunnier climates (thank you, Florida, for spoiling me).

Hopefully it goes without being said that the weather in the south of England can't be compared to the weather in the north of Scotland, but the general rule is that the further north you get, the colder temperatures you will encounter.

However, the UK isn't known for "extreme" weather. The summers are warm and the winters are cool, but it is not common for it to get too far below freezing nor scorching hot. It does snow occasionally in the winters, but it's very rare for it to be heavy and when it is, the southern part of the UK definitely shuts down because they're unable to cope.

It's not likely that you'll encounter really massive natural occurrences like earthquakes or hurricanes or tornados, but you will learn how to keep your house from getting too damp and the importance of having a quality waterproof jacket!

When Brits talk about weather (and they will, often – it's great small talk), they'll also refer to the temperature in Celsius instead of Fahrenheit. This takes some getting used to at first, and has led to some very confusing moments as I tried to figure out how it could possibly be "23 degrees" in the middle of July.

There is a specific calculation you can make to translate Celsius into Fahrenheit, but I was never very good at math, so I have just tried to memorize the "main" temperatures like freezing and boiling and then try and guesstimate from there.

If you want to get more specific than a wild guess, you can use the formula that suggests you multiple the temperature in Celsius by two, and then add 30. This should get you relatively close to the Fahrenheit temperature.

The one thing that really caught me off guard about the weather in the UK had less to do with what was falling down from the sky (or not) and more to do with how many daylight hours there would be. When you look at a world map, you'll see that the UK is "higher" than all of the US except Alaska, meaning it's further from the equator. Because of this, the daylight hours vary a lot more throughout the year.

In practicality, this means that in the winter, it can get dark very early. On the darkest day of the year, December 21st, the sun rises at about 8am and it sets just before 4pm. On the longest day of the year, June 23rd, the sun will rise before 5am and sets a bit after 9pm.

It takes a while to get your body used to these different daylight patterns, and you'll soon discover your "favorite time of year" for the daylight hours (yes, there is such a thing). I would have thought that the longest days would be my favorite, but it was also very unnatural for me to hear the birds chirping and sun streaming through my window at 4:45am and was a real adjustment to figure out how to sleep through it!

Currency

Instead of dollars and cents, the UK has pounds and pence. They refer to "bills" as "notes," and they have a five pound note, a ten pound note, a twenty pound note, and a fifty pound note. Unlike American bills, all of the UK note denominations are slightly different sizes.

For coins, you have one pence, two pence, five pence, ten pence, twenty pence, fifty pence, one pound, and two pounds. "Pence" is shortened to "p" in conversation, so you could tell someone that your item cost "57 p" as well.

These are also all different sizes and varying shades of color so they are easier to tell apart.

Pence are related to pounds in the same way that cents are related to the dollar – there are 100 pence to each pound.

Because the smaller denominations in pounds are in coins rather than bill or note form, you will find your purse or bag a bit more jangly than in America! I tend to try to use these up first to avoid feeling like a bank robber.

Credit and debit cards are widely used throughout the UK, and other methods of payments like Apple Pay are also available in many of the larger cities and more established stores.

Pound notes are issued by the Bank of England, as well as authorized banks in Scotland and Northern Ireland. The Bank of England notes are what you will encounter in England, Wales, and often in Scotland and Northern Ireland as well, while the Scottish notes and Northern Irish notes are only really circulated and used in their respective countries.

You can sometimes use Scottish notes and Northern Irish notes in England and in the other UK countries, but often the stores and cashiers will not want to take them. Whether you live in Scotland or Northern Ireland or are just visiting, the easiest idea is to use up your Scottish or Northern Irish notes in that country and then use the Bank of England notes after those are gone.

Politics

After living in the UK for seven years, I still don't understand the political structure fully, and after the absolute mess that is and was Brexit, I'm not entirely sure the Brits do either!

To help give you the briefest of background so you can read articles and talk to Brits with at least some semblance understanding, I'm going to outline how the UK government operates, and leave you to figure out the rest.

And if you do, let me know!

Understanding National Government

The UK is a constitutional monarchy, which means that there is a Prime

Minister and a Queen. The Queen is "Head of State," which means that while she does have the ultimate power over some things, she is not actually running the day-to-day workings of the government. That is the job of the Prime Minister, who is head of the government.

The Queen or King is not elected, and instead this role is passed down through the Royal Family.

The Prime Minister, however, is voted on by members of his or her own political party. The public does not have a direct vote as to who the Prime Minister is, but instead they vote for the political party.

UK elections have to happen every five years, but they usually happen more often than that because there are other circumstances that allow elections to take place.

The political party system tends to be less of a "two party" system than in the US. Well-known parties include the Conservative party, the Labour party, the Liberal Democrats, the Green Party, and some of the very right wing parties like UKIP.

I used to think it was possible to "compare" these parties to US ones and say that the Conservative party are like Republicans and the Labour party are like Democrats. This may be true on the absolute surface, but once you start digging deeper, you find that it's not possible to compare parties in two different countries with different cultures and views on religion, social issues, and the economy.

As an American expat, you won't be able to vote for at least five years until you qualify for citizenship, so take that time to pay attention to the parties and see which one you align with!

In the UK Parliament, which operates from London, there are two main houses: the House of Lords and the House of Commons. The House of Lords are appointed by the Queen, not elected. The House of Commons are elected in the sense that they are the local representatives from across the UK whose party has won the most recent election in that area. These representatives are referred to as "Members of Parliament" or "MP"s for short.

Understanding Local Government

I also want to quickly mention the terminology behind even more local administrations, as there are "councils" and "councillors," and the first time I heard about "councillors" I thought my friend was telling me that she was going to write to her therapist.

A "council" is basically a local administration of a town or a collection of towns and villages that manages things like recycling and waste, neighbour disputes, new building works and more. Your local council is based on your address. A "councillor" is the person who is supposed to act as the go-between between the residents and the council, effectively advocating for the needs of the residents and representing them on a larger scale.

This hopefully helps explain a term you will or have run into, "council tax." This is a yearly fee (often paid in monthly installments) that you must pay to your local council that covers things like recycling, waste management, local libraries, fire departments, roads, etc.

Quality over Quantity
The Art of Making Friends as an Expat

"It's not easy."

Making friends as an expat in Britain is different for everyone, but that's the main mantra that gets repeated in expat groups time and time again.

Note, the phrase isn't, "it's impossible," but simply that it's "not as easy as you might think."

But then, no one said expat life was easy. They just said it was going to be worth it. Or that you have to do it because your job is making you move or your British husband is going through a mid-life crisis and wants to go back home or whatever the case may be.

Before I get into my experience making friends in the UK (or not, you'll have to wait and see), let's dive into one of my most vivid memories in the UK.

Settle in and picture this.

It's raining, dark, and cold. So it was like, December in England. Or February. Or, heck, maybe it was July, the British weather could mean it was basically any time of year.

But, anyway, I'm walking next to a darkened field after a trivial fight with my husband about something or other. As I plod one foot in front of the other, I think about who might jump out of the bush to murder me and wonder if it would make the news and then I walk a bit faster and THEN, instead of letting my mind get carried away with the thoughts of where they would store my body, I figure that the best thing to do to distract myself from the fight with my husband and also my impending doom would be to call my mom or my friends back in America to talk.

Of course, the time difference meant that they're at work, but I thought that if you don't try, you don't get. And also, surely me calling is like the bat signal that tells them they need to drop whatever they're doing and pick up now because I'm in distress and I'm like five minutes away from stopping by the store and buying myself a tub of overpriced Ben and Jerry's.

The first number I dialed was my Mom's.

Ring ring ring. The rain was getting heavier now and continued to hit me and soak my phone.

Ring ring ring.

No answer.

I huff a little, but got my spirits up by dialing the number of my best friend.

Ring ring ring

Again, no answer. I didn't immediately pin this on her because she worked at Target at the time and might have been on a shift selling people the dream of feeling fancy in a way only suburbia can, but whatever the reason, she was not on the other end of the line.

Now I'm getting increasingly distraught, realizing that I am basically all alone in the world and am going to die alone in a rainy field and no one will come to my funeral, and - I stop myself and dial the next number of another friend.

Ring ring ring.

I bet you can guess what happened next.

She picked up and we had an amazing conversation about my feelings and how much I missed her and then I felt so much better.

NOT.

No answer, again.

At this point, I gave up, had slowed my canter back down to a walk as I cried the whole way home on the point of an epic expat meltdown.

While reading this now, you might think this is a clear sign that I needed some, shall we say, perspective, but at the time it was just confirmation that I had no friends, no hope, and nothing to my name besides some soggy shoelaces and a life of regret.

Sorry, perspective – what's that?!

Back to my introduction to this chapter – the general consensus among American expats in the UK is that making friends is difficult. People's experiences cover a wide range, obviously, but let's just say there are no group chats I've ever participated in or seen where everyone is just raving about how easy it is to make friends as an expat in the UK.

If you haven't moved abroad yet, you're probably terrified at this point, and so I want to stop and tell you – dude, breathe, this is not as scary as it seems, and this isn't to say that you can't make friends in the UK or won't. It just comes with different sets of things to think about, which I'll address soon so grab your most comforting blanket and soldier on!

If you are currently an expat in the UK, I'm imagining you're nodding along and raising your hand up towards the sky yelling, "PREACH!"

Or maybe you're just gently nodding because you're British now and don't do loud proclamations.

There are a few different points to touch on when talking about making friends as an expat in the UK, because so much of the topic can't be discussed without acknowledging a few basic principles.

Firstly, let's talk about making friends as an adult, because this is a worldwide phenomenon that doesn't only plague expats. It's just that often, as expats, we are leaving our childhood or lifelong friends behind in the US, and so we are forced to make new friends as an adult if we want to live our best lives in the UK, rather than always having to rely on our friends in the US answering their phones.

Making friends as an adult is a whole ordeal that comes with way more rules than childhood friendships born from proximity and a similar interest in green Play-Doh. And I don't mean to sound negative when I say "ordeal," but it just is. In the same way that cleaning our house is an ordeal or interviewing for the job we want is an ordeal. Just because the end result is something we desire doesn't mean it's all fun and games while we're doing it.

See, not only do we tend to have less time than we did as children to just hang around and get to know what kind of Kool-Aid someone drinks (both literally and figuratively), but we also have this self-awareness that we lacked as kids. While a child, or perhaps yourself as a college freshmen, might bound into the next door neighbor's house and scream, "HELLO MY NAME IS TOMMY DO YOU WANT TO PLAY LEGOS WITH ME," we can't quite do the same as adults – though don't quote me on that as I haven't tried. Instead, we feel we need to present ourselves a certain way to be liked or seen as worthy of hanging out with.

We also forget, as adults, that some of our best friendships as children or young adults were built over years and years of mutual affection, trust, hard times, good times, days driving around town doing nothing, dinner dates at Chipotle, whatever it is. Genuine, lifelong, "I'll cover for you if you murder someone" friendships take time, and even if you're the world's biggest extrovert, there's no way around this.

Why do we get so down on ourselves and annoyed then when we can't immediately have the same level of friendships with those around us in the UK? As I was frantically dialing my best friend's number on that overdramatic night, I was consumed with thoughts that I had no friends because I didn't have friends in the UK *like her*. And seeing how we had known each other for 24 years at that point, it's no real shock to a rational mind, is it?

Now, the second thing we need to talk about is making friends with Brits and the culture around friendships here, as not only do we get to navigate the adult-friendship making, but we get to do it in another country where the attitudes towards friendships and where to find them are not always the same as we're used to.

And yes, I say "get to," because you know what, as much as Americans can find making friends in the UK a struggle, our lives are richer and more full for having the opportunity to have lived in at least two different countries, and we've all got to pull together and try our hardest to see through those bleak times when you're crying in a field about your life, you know?

For full disclosure, so you can weigh in your mind whether or not you'll be better at making friends than me, I am an introvert by nature. I enjoy having a small group of close friends rather than a wide net, and I prefer genuine conversation over dinner to parties.

I also find it incredibly tedious to get to that part of a friendship because I find the beginning small talk awkward and uncomfortable. Unfortunately for me, in some cases, this small talk is really the way to start a friendship in the UK and it may go on a lot longer than you would expect it to – not just in terms of your first meeting, but your second, your third, your fourth – five years down the line you may just be getting around to where the person grew up.

I exaggerate, but only slightly.

Now, before I continue, I do want to reiterate that I am only summarizing the basic "problems" that Americans seem to run into when trying to make friends in the UK, not speaking for every single American or every single British person.

Overall, though, there's just something a bit slower about friendship with Brits, not because they aren't friendly but because they don't wear their heart on their sleeves, usually. When we make friends in America, it's often enough to strike up a conversation with someone in the grocery store line who lives nearby and then suddenly you're around their house for dinner and talking about the vacation you're going on together next month.

With Brits, you probably wouldn't say anything at all in the checkout line, for starters, but even if you saw someone in that same line every day for a year, you'd spend the first six months talking about the weather and traffic, a couple months acknowledging that the other person has kids but not asking about them, and then maybe by the final three you would know the children's names and possibly have an invite over for tea at some unspecified time in the future that probably wouldn't happen until the following year.

This slower friendship timeline is compounded when you realize that, as American expats, we are desperate to make friends and perhaps overly enthusiastic about the process. Brits, on the other hand, from a cultural perspective, seem to not be allowed to show their enthusiasm about most things for fear that they'll seem, well, American.

So here we are, the American golden retrievers, trying to make friends with the British tabby cats, and sometimes it might come off to them like we're trying to jump on them and lick their face off while they're still trying to tentatively decide if they're okay being in the same room as us.

It can be a recipe for disaster, on both ends of the spectrum, but there is a way forward.

Introverts – Try Your Best!

Much of my problems making friends in the UK has been giving into my introverted tendencies. On a good day, I prefer people to start up conversations with me rather than the other way around, so put me in Britain and I'm more than happy to awkwardly ignore the person sitting next to me at a dinner just the same as they are with me.

But if you're going to have any success in making British friends, past experience shows that often you should be the one making the first move, opening the lines of communication. Muster up all of the courage inside you to just bring up any form of small talk, ask them a question about something you already know the answer to, compliment their shoes – whatever it is, try your best to push yourself out of your lovely, quiet comfort zone you have set for yourself.

If all else fails, find an extrovert to introduce you to people. My husband is a confident socializer and loves talking, so I invite him to events with me for the sole purpose of using him both as a socializing shield for when it becomes too much and to make him introduce me to random strangers that neither of us know.

Prioritize Friend Making

Friend making can be hard work. It's a mission in and of itself, and between my commute of two and a half hours a day each way on a weekday and my desire to just completely shut the world out on a weekend, it can be hard to prioritize it in my life.

The problem is, you get out of life what you put into it. I still have a job because I show up the vast majority of the time and do the work expected of me. My blog is thriving because I spend countless hours working on it. I've seen the entire series of Gilmore Girls about 67 times because I put the time into watching the episodes over and over again.

It's the same way with making friends. If you don't put the time in to engage with people and go to events and put yourself out there, you're not going to get much back.

Don't Just Stick to Expats

My biggest mistake in making friends in the UK has been gravitating only towards other expats, whether from America or all over the world. In some cases it's worked out with people who have ended up staying long term like me. In other cases, it seems like by the time I've actually made a new friend they've gone and moved away, leaving me to start the process all over again.

Now, I am absolutely not saying that you shouldn't make friends with other expats. My expat friends have been invaluable in my life and there's nothing like going to dinner and spending the entire night going, "YES! YOU GET ME!"

That being said, don't let it stop you from trying to make friends with Brits as well. No, you're not always going to be on the same page and yes, sometimes they're going to make references to a television show from their childhood that completely goes over your head, but try to diversify your friend group as much as possible and be open to friendships outside of your expat circle.

Be the One to Invite

One of the biggest downfalls of any American expat in the UK trying to make friends is waiting for invitations to roll in. Do not just sit back and hope that you are noticed and will be invited places. It's not because people don't like you, but as mentioned before, sometimes there is this idea in Britain that inviting someone somewhere is putting a burden on them to say "yes" or to inconvenience them somehow. What Americans would view as friendly and welcoming, a Brit might view as uncomfortable and encroaching in your personal space.

So don't wait for them. Send the invitations yourself! Start small, with individual friendships, so that they can't hide behind the shared responsibility of a group invite. Say, "Hey Tony, my husband and I would love to have you and Sarah around for dinner – let us know what dates work for you!" or "Hey Georgia, I'm taking Tabitha (pretend that's your child) to see *Dumbo* on Friday night – would you and Cindy Lou Who (that's her kid) want to join us?"

If you invite and invite and invite and that particular person never answers or responds affirmatively without at least an attempt at an excuse, then that's fine – you can't win them all. But what you will probably find is that the more you do the inviting and the more times you invite someone somewhere, the faster they will open up and then start also inviting you places.

Use Any Common Ground – at all

Now, I don't mean that you should just approach a stranger off the street because you both have blonde hair and try to start a friendship over it. Instead of forcing a "common ground," try and put yourself in situations where you will automatically share a common ground with people.

This could mean trying to make friends at work, where at least you'll all be in the same field and maybe have the same passions/complaints about the boss.

It could mean volunteering for a cause and making friends who are also interested in the same things you are, whether that's caring for the elderly or fostering adorable little puppies.

If there is a church nearby (and there always is, this is the UK, come on), go get involved in the social events even if you're not religious for the sake of making friends who live in the same area as you. This goes for any faith community, really, as you're going to find that people in these situations are in a position where they are more naturally open to welcoming you in to whatever is going on.

If you're a parent, you're in luck as I'm repeatedly told by women that the easiest way to make friends as an expat in the UK is to have a child.

Apparently, having a child allows you to participate in prenatal classes with other soon-to-be parents in your area. And if you don't make friends there, there's still your child's school years to join the PTA and get close to other parents.

Unfortunately for my friend making skills, having a kid is definitely not in the cards anytime soon for me, and I'm not willing to have one to benefit my social circle, but to anyone else who can take advantage of these friendship circles – go for it!

This also applies to those with pets – nothing like letting your little Rover make friends for you while you're out walking him every morning. Brits might be scared of Americans who act like golden retrievers, but they're much more interested in actual golden retrievers!

Give it Time

It would be disingenuous to propose that you are going to go to one meet-up of "People who Love Taylor Swift in the South of England" and suddenly come away with all of your new best friends.

Even if you use all of the advice above, it still takes time to really develop anything that we, as Americans, would consider a "close friendship," and sometimes American expats still feel that they just haven't achieved the same "friendship level" in the amount of time they could have done in the States.

And you know what, that's okay. Be patient, focus on the social acquaintances or friends you do have and make time for yourself to pursue individual passions that you might have or self-care routines like running, writing, reading, crafting.

Maintain Relationships with Your American Friends

One of the hardest parts about living abroad, for me, has been the lack of ability to see some of my best friends in person as often as I would like. Sure, many of my friends have moved far away from my hometown and are all spread out, but it would definitely be easier to take a two hour flight to Texas from Florida than a 12 hour one from the UK. If you have a close group of friends in your local area who still hang out and are going on with their lives without you, it can be even more difficult to be a whole ocean away.

When I work with study abroad students who are only coming for a short term or a semester at most, I encourage them to not prioritize their American friends over their life in the UK for the time being. After all, I say, you only have a limited amount of time here, and your friends will always be there when you see them again in four months.

For expats, my advice is the opposite – maintain those American friendships for all that they're worth, going the extra mile to stay in touch and keep those lines of communication open.

It's a challenge, for sure. Between time zone differences and busy lives, it can feel like you're slowly drifting away from the people you love the most because of your geographical differences, but fight against it. Text more often, make Skype dates and hold yourself to them, stay up an hour later on a Tuesday night to call if that's the only time they're available.

These friendships represent your "old life" in America, the person you were before moving to the UK. And while living your new expat life and settling in to new surroundings is important, the "old you" is equally important and deserves to continue enjoying the things that have always made you, "you."

This is not a case of "simply drop everyone and everything in the US, you don't live there anymore." No, you worked hard to develop those relationships, to become the person that you are now because of what you experienced or loved or went through in the States and the people you went through those things with. Own that and nurture those friendships as much as possible.

If you really work at it, don't ghost them every time they text you (okay, I'm the worst at this), and actually stick to your word of still being a friend to them even from around the world, distance is no problem at all when it comes to maintaining those bonds. I have people in my life I haven't seen for three, four, or five years and I know that they would still be there for me if I needed it.

And if you ever do struggle with your friendship making skills in the UK, just remember that at the end of the day, friendship is all about quality over quantity. You could have a million friends and still feel all alone, or you can focus your energy into growing and developing the ones you do have in the UK, no matter what stage they're at.

Even if that means being best friends with the puppy who lives across the street because he's excited to see you every time you walk out the door – you run with that beautiful canine friendship and make it count!

Why the World Needs More Mixer Taps

Getting Cozy at Home in the UK

When I bought my first house, which happened to be a mid-terraced house in the UK, I sent my grandma a picture of the outside.

In the picture, it also showed the other two houses on either side of us. I assumed that she would know those were other houses, but I was suspicious when she replied, "Oh, Kalyn! That is AMAZING! I'm so proud of you" in a way that seemed to mean that she thought I was the next Bill Gates and owned the entire complex I was showing her.

"Oh," I said, sheepishly. "No, Grammy, I just own that tiny sliver of the house in the middle! The other doors go to my neighbors!"

"Oh!" she said, and we laughed and laughed as I died a slow painful death on the inside when I thought about how much more I could have gotten for my money in the suburbs of Orlando where I grew up.

My grandma, like many Americans, aren't used to the concept that a house could actually be connected to other houses, partly because we don't call them "terraced houses," we call them "townhouses" and partly because we don't usually have a concept of housing prices anywhere but our local area – much less another country. To think that I owned basically the whole street made sense to her, both in a supportive grandmotherly way because she thought I was much more accomplished than I was and in an "anything is possible" American mindset.

As it turns out, my two bedroom house in the UK is smaller in square feet than my friend's studio apartment in Dallas, but that's just the way life is here – condensed. Oh, and also, expensive.

Now, this is all relative, because property prices do differ in the UK, but the overall experience of many American expats who move to the UK is, "Holy &*(!, why does this 10 square foot shed cost more than my dinky student apartment in the most run down part of my American college town?

Considering the US is about 40 times larger than the UK, it makes sense that everything is a bit more crammed and that the demand for housing means that the prices are generally higher.

But I'm not here to get into the sociological or political motives behind UK housing, developers, and building in the UK.

I'm here to tell you that your house or flat (the word for apartment in the UK) may be smaller than you're used to, and that is just the way of the world.

I also think it's important that we talk about the ways in which actual homes and buildings are different in the UK than in the US, because a home is a sanctuary and there's nothing that destroys your confidence more than realizing you don't even know how to turn on the light in the bathroom or flush the toilet.

Yes, how to flush the toilet! It's different! Who even knew?!

To talk about homes and buildings in the UK, I'd like to take you on a tour of my imaginary demonstration house so we can go room by room and discuss what's different. Pretend I'm a real estate agent, except I'm not trying to sell you on why open floor plans are totally in now or why this neighborhood will be great for your currently non-existent kids.

If you haven't moved to the UK yet, then take notes! If you are already here, then I hope you feel supported in your hatred for non-mixer taps because I see you, I feel you, and I am WITH you.

The Entrance

When you first walk into my imaginary house, you might immediately notice that there are two or more floors. It is highly, highly common in the UK for houses to have multiple floors. In Florida and other hot climates, we mostly have just one floor because, well, heat rises and that's one thing we don't need more of!

In the UK, on the other hand, homes are built to keep *IN* the heat, and so multiple stories doesn't phase them. It's also a handy way to fit more homes into an area that is already small – build up, not out!

If you do come across a single story home, it's referred to as a "bungalow," which created a lot of confusion the first time my husband pointed one out.

"I'd like a bungalow like that one day," he said, pointing to a single story home.

I looked at it, confused, trying to figure out what he meant.

"What makes it a bungalow?" I asked.

"It's just got one floor," he said. "What would you call it?"

"Oh," I replied. "I'd call it a…house."

Once we came to terms that what we both thought of as "normal" for a house differed, we proceeded to explore the other vocabulary surrounding UK homes.

The first actually has to do with the floors of a house (or any building). Brits refer to the first floor as the "ground floor," which makes the second floor the first floor and so on and so forth. This is one of those small tidbits that you should store away in the back of your brain for when you go to your first job interview in the UK and the receptionist tells you to head up to the second floor. Being on the wrong floor and waiting for your interviewer to show up for the first ten to fifteen minutes of your interview is not a good look.

Allegedly.

As I mentioned, homes can either be "terraced" or "detached." If it's detached, that means it doesn't share walls with any other homes and you could physically walk around just that house from the outside.

If a home is terraced, it means it shares walls with other homes in a row. If it's surrounded on two sides, it's a "mid-terrace," and if it's at the end of the row, it's called – brace yourselves – "end of terrace."

But wait! It doesn't stop there!

If you have just two homes that share a joining wall, these are referred to as "semi-detached."

And if you're like, *hey Kalyn, remember how we talked about property prices in the UK earlier? Yeah, well, I don't have a house – I'm in an apartment because houses in the UK cost like 8 trillion dollars!*

Oh, yeah! Apartments! Called "flats" in the UK, these are a popular type of accommodation for loads of people in major cities, just like in the US. There are purpose-built flats like apartment complexes, as well as flats that are transformed houses and flats built above stores (or shops, as they're known here – more on that later).

There are also "maisonettes," which are basically apartments with their own exterior entrances (mostly converted houses which have been split into two or more).

No matter what kind of home you find yourself in while in the UK, it's important to make it feel your own. Whether you're renting, buying, or perhaps living with a friend or family member, creating your own little cocoon of personal space does wonders for life as an expat and gives you a sense of control over what's going on around you.

With that in mind, please – come in further to my house so I can walk you through the weird and mysterious ways of non-mixer taps, washing up bowls, and heated towel rails!

Oh, but before you do – notice that slot in the front door? That's for the mail. Mailboxes as a separate structure in your front yard is not the done thing in the UK – instead it's "posted" directly through what is referred to as a "letter box" that is built directly into the front door. The trade off for not having to walk down the driveway to get your mail is that sometimes the sound of mail thudding through your front door unexpectedly is enough to make you jump.

And when I say jump, I mean that I have shot up out of my chair at times, heart pounding and ready to face the intruder who was halfway in the house, only to realize it was just a bunch of bills.

The Living Areas

As you walk in the living room, I'll first have you know that in the UK, most people call it the "lounge." There is not much specifically about living rooms in the UK that differ from the US, so I thought I'd point out a few things that you may see throughout the home that are different (or called different things).

For our first exhibit, come on over to one of the electrical outlets (and don't stick your fingers in).

The first thing you'll notice is that the actual plug is different – instead of two main holes, you've got three in the shape of a triangle. This means that anything you plug in in the UK only goes one way - there is a right way, and there is a "this is not going to work no matter how hard you try way." My husband calls American plugs, "those stupid two prong teeth things that always fall out," and he wanted to make sure I included that in the book so his feelings on American plugs are loud and clear.

The most important thing to know about UK outlets, though, doesn't even have to do with the actual plug, but actually the switch located next to the plug.

I had never thought about this before, but in the States, the electricity is basically constantly flowing to the plug. There is no "on" or "off," there is only the constant fear that your toddler will stick a knife into it out of curiosity and end up with their hair singed off.

In the UK, they had the forethought to put in a switch that can turn off the electricity flowing to that specific plug. This means that to make anything "work" you need to make sure the switch is to the "on" position when you plug your device in. Electricity prices in the UK are often higher than in the US, and Brits are culturally more eco-sensitive. This lends itself to more in-built ways to not waste energy around the house.

That being said, the number of times I have forgotten the simple rule of British plugs and ended up waking up in the morning to a completely dead phone that I thought was charging overnight is too many to count!

Now that we've finished our discussion all about plugs and you really need a rest, I'd invite you to come sit down on my couch, but I can't.

Well, I can, but in the UK, couches are often referred to as "sofas" (which is also not uncommon in many areas in the US) or "settees".

The Kitchen

Hey, are you thirsty from all of this house talk? Why don't you come into the kitchen with me and I'll get you a glass of water while you mule this over?

As we walk into the kitchen, you might notice that the fridge is not nearly the same size as the ones you're used to in America. Even if a UK home has a "full size" fridge, it will often still be much smaller than you might be used to in an "American" size fridge. Every time we are in America, my husband is horrified at the sheer size of our fridges and wonders how someone could possibly fill one up.

I keep trying to explain to him that the answer is Costco, but I'm not sure he'll ever get used to it.

If I were British, I'd offer you a cup of tea and you would politely accept even if you didn't want it, but I haven't quite gotten the taste for tea ever. So, instead, I'll just point out that electric tea kettles are in almost every UK home, and not only are they used to boil the water for tea, but people also boil water in the kettle before then putting it on to boil on the stove.

Oh, and there's another thing – seriously, the kitchen is just fraught with "oh, and another thing!" – the stove isn't called the stove in the UK. It's called the hob. Rhymes with Bob. Stoves are often either gas or electric in the UK, with a preference for gas.

When I open my oven to show you the cake I've been making for you, you also might notice that the oven looks slightly different than you might be used to.

Many ovens in the UK are comprised of the "grill" up top and then the main oven compartment down below. The grill is similar to what Americans would call the broiler – it sends heat down from the top only, rather than cooking from underneath. Brits would usually refer to an outside grill as a barbecue.

Suddenly, I realize that I need to wash some plates off because I'm a slob and they're all dirty, so I turn to the sink and you might notice that it's smaller than the large double sinks many American homes have. Instead, it might just be one sink or it might be a "sink and a half," with one regular sized sink and then a very small half sink to the side that's both thinner and less deep.

My British friends contend that the reason for the lack of double sinks is the lack of space, which I would agree with, but their argument for the "half sink" being at all useful is because they can pour the leftover tea or other drinks into it even if they have the main sink full of the "washing up," as they would say. Or you can wash vegetables or something in it even if you have the main sink full.

I can sort of see this explanation, but let's just say that the first thing I insisted on when we remodelled our kitchen was a full double sink, and my husband is now a true convert.

You also might notice a bucket in the sink. This is all hypothetical as these "washing up bowls" as they're called are the bane of my British existence, but let's just pretend for right now that I have one.

Many, many homes in the UK have these bowls, and they use them to wash dishes. Instead of filling up the entire sink with water, they will fill up this bowl with soap and water and wash the dishes with it.

The problem that I have always found with these bowls is that they constantly live in the sink – they're always there, taunting you by the space they're taking up, and you never truly feel like you have ownership of the entire sink because that stupid bowl is just staring at you with its smudged plastic and the leftovers of last night's dinner.

Oh, and speaking of last night's dinner – don't put it down the garbage disposal, because have I mentioned there isn't one? Be sure to put any food waste into the garbage can (called a bin in the UK).

The last British oddity in the layout of the kitchen that I feel it's important to mention is that there is a high chance your washing machine and/or dryer will be there! This isn't the case for every house – some do have what they would call a "utility" or what we would call a "laundry room," but because of the smaller nature of homes here, many times there isn't any room for such luxuries!

Instead, your washing machine will just be in your kitchen like it's no big deal, and there is a very good chance it's a side loading one that loads from the front rather than the top. Brits that come to the States are often confounded by how big our washing machines are in our homes.

And, get this – sometimes you won't have a separate dryer, but instead a combi washer/dryer. I KNOW, BLOWING YOUR AMERICAN MIND.

The dryer component of these combi machines doesn't often work spectacularly well, but then again, many Brits don't even see a need for the dryer for most of the year. The culture here is very much to hang up your clothes to dry, whether that's outside on the "washing line," or inside on a "drying rack" or clothes horse.

I have never truly understood this, given that many months of the year in the UK are cold and rainy, which are not ideal for drying clothes, but the act of using Mother Nature to dry your clothes as best as possible is widespread and isn't going anywhere any time soon.

The Bathroom

If you have to use the bathroom while you're in my British house, you'll first have to learn that Brits often call it the "toilet" or the "loo" rather than a "bathroom" or "restroom." In fact, one time my mom asked where the restroom was in a supermarket here, and the woman looked at her quizzically as she thought my mom wanted somewhere to…rest.

In a home, there are a few things you'll notice about a UK bathroom that's different from ones in the States. Firstly, to turn the light on, you'll either turn on a switch on the outside of the door or there will be a string pull cord on the inside. There are UK building regulations that usually prevents a switch from being on the interior of a bathroom.

This also means that there is not going to be a plug in your bathroom – you know how in America you can just plug in your hair dryer and go to town while standing in front of the bathroom mirror? Those days are no more in the UK!

You can have a "shaver point" socket, but not a regular plug, again due to electrical regulations.

Now that you've actually figured out where the light switch is and have made it into the bathroom, you may notice that there isn't a lock on the door. Many home bathrooms in the UK do not have locks, and instead you're supposed to take the door being closed as sign that someone is in there.

This is fine, until you sit outside the bathroom at your parents-in-law's house for like 20 minutes because you're pretty sure no one is in there, but the door is closed and you're too scared to knock.

You'll also see a rail structure on one of the walls that has towels hanging on it. This is the amazing invention of the "heated towel rail," which can be found in many homes and is where you would keep your current towel when you're not using it. The towel rail will heat up to both dry off and warm your towels so that you can be sure you're not just letting moldy towels fester in the depths of winter when it's cold and damp outside.

Another difference which takes some Americans by surprise is the button to flush the toilet! Sometimes there are handles like the ones we would see in the States, and the thing to know with these is that you often have to hold them down for a while before it flushes. Like, an eternity.

More commonly, however, is more of a push button system, either in a circle or square shape. There will be one smaller circle within a larger circle, both pushable. The larger button will send more water through the toilet and produce a more full flush, and you can guess what you should use that for.

It also comes as a shock how low the water fills up to in a British toilet after you flush. And whatever you sent down that drain…it's going to the "mains." Most British homes are connected to the main waste systems, not septic tanks.

And now that I've talked about toilets and waste way too much for my liking, let's move on!

When you go to wash your hands, it's likely that you may come across two separate faucets (called 'taps' in the UK), one for cold and one for hot. There is no real method to the madness here in terms of how you're supposed to wash your hands without either scalding yourself or freezing your fingers off – I sometimes turn on both and quickly switch my hands between the flows, but this isn't always ideal when you're trying to keep it simple and not waste water.

The reason for this is due to the old plumbing systems. It was considered unsafe to have hot and cold water mixed together, as they came from different places and the hot water was often not fit to drink.

Increasingly, as new homes get built and plumbing updated, mixer taps, where you can have both hot and cold flow through one faucet, are more common and much appreciated by the American expat community.

If you need to take a shower or bath while you're going through this real estate walkthrough (which would be very strange, but just go with it), you might notice that a British showerhead is often detachable and able to move up down, compared to the American showerheads which are mostly fixed to the wall.

The standard size for a bathtub is also slightly different, with longer ones being more common in the UK and shorter sizes being more prevalent in

America. If you want to know how I know this, it has something to do with the time my British husband decided to redo our entire bathroom based off what he learned on HGTV's *Fixer Upper*. Enough said.

I've also noticed that while most American homes I've lived in have on-demand hot water in the shower, a few British places I've stayed in have hot water tanks that take a while to fill up. That means that if just one or two people shower, all of the hot water can be gone until the next cycle. This is something to keep in mind when you move into your new place – figure out how your shower works and whether you need to time your showers appropriately or have the freedom to shower with reckless abandon!

The Bedroom

If I'm feeling like I want to give you the full house tour, I may show you our bedroom and office, which may look similar to what you would picture a bedroom or office looking like in America (despite the smaller square footage).

You will notice a couple of things though – one being that if you're from a warm climate like I am, the lack of a ceiling fan will stick out to you! Coming from Florida, I was just used to a ceiling fan being an essential part of any bedroom, but here they aren't common in the slightest. When it does get hot, people will just try to leave their windows open and perhaps drag their standing fan out from the closet.

If you see a bed in the room and want to ask me about the bed size, you should also be aware that they differ from American sizes. For a brief rundown, a US "Twin" is called a "Single" in the UK, a "Double" is called a "Full," a US "Queen" is a UK "King" and a US "King" is a UK "Superking." And the holy grail of US beds, a California king? That doesn't exist in the UK! These sizes are also rough, there might be a couple of inches difference in comparing the bedsizes, but it gives you a good idea of what to expect.

There is also different language when it comes to what is put on the bed. Americans often have a comforter over a top sheet and a fitted sheet. In the UK, you'll usually just find a fitted sheet with a "duvet" on top. Unlike a comforter that is just one piece, a duvet is basically a basic comforter covered by a "duvet cover" which is the consistency of a sheet.

If you've ever had trouble putting a fitted sheet on the bed, please let me introduce you to the absolute hell that is putting on a duvet cover. There are multiple methods, including turning the cover inside out, climbing into it, and then putting it on the corners of the duvet and essentially flipping it right side out. Other people try to finagle it on by the help of gravity and standing on the bed while letting the duvet drop into the duvet cover.

If you're like me, you take the route of flailing on the bed for like ten minutes before your British other half walks in and goes, "what in the world are you doing? Give me that" and then does it for you.

Is your head thoroughly spinning now? Good, that means you're having the authentic expat experience. Moving on swiftly!

Another area where you may notice a difference is the windows! Many American homes have screens on their windows to keep insects out when you have the windows open, but not in the UK! Seeing a screen on a window is very very uncommon – when you have the window open, you invite the whole of the insect world in.

This is usually not a huge problem – the breeze that you get through a wide open window is excellent at times, but I've spent more than my fair share of days chasing flies and hornets around the house with the hose of a vacuum cleaner because they couldn't resist coming inside and exploring.

And it has to be mentioned, when you're lying awake on those hot July nights with an ice pack on your pillow, it may have already occurred to you – air conditioning is absolutely not standard in UK homes. Less than 1% of UK homes have air conditioning, compared to 80+ percent in the US. Again, this is down to the lack of a need for it, though in recent years the summers have been scorching and perhaps leading more households to purchase portable air conditioners. Central air, though? Not happening anytime soon!

As for the heating, when the weather gets cold (which is will, this is the UK after all!) the heating in homes is provided by radiators, not HVAC. Instead of the air being heated, the heat in the home comes from heated water that flows around the home. There are also electric heating systems, as well as portable oil heaters, but this largely depends on the home or flat you live in and what is necessary.

Airing Cupboard, Hallways, Closets and More

Before we move on to the outside of the house, I wanted to mention some other random differences you might hear about or find in a UK home.

Firstly, there is often a closet either in a bedroom or in a hallway called the "airing cupboard." This is where the hot water tank would be stored and might have shelves where families may put some clothes like underwear or socks to keep them warm and dry.

You should also know that what an American calls a "closet," a Brit would call a "cupboard." And a cupboard that holds clothes is called a "wardrobe."

Another random quirk is that Brits often call hallways just "halls."

And that space at the top of the house that Americans call an "attic?" That's what Brits call the "loft." A "loft" in the UK is somewhere at the very top of the house where you store the junk you don't want, not the more trendy-sounding "chill out" space that many Americans would think of when we refer to a loft.

Outside the Home

As you politely make your exit from my house and I stand in the doorway talking to you for about a million years because I've become too British to know how to say goodbye quickly, take a look around the outside of the house. You'll notice that the front yard (called a "front garden") is probably smaller than many in America, and it may or may not have a driveway (called a "drive"). If it doesn't have a driveway, people will just park on the street in front of their houses and get into neighborhood squabbles over who parks where.

Around the back, there may be the backyard, called the "back garden" or "garden." This isn't to be confused with an actual vegetable or flower garden, as the word "garden" basically just refers to the space outside that house that can include just grass or flowers, vegetable patches, etc.

For a long time, I kept hearing people referring to the "gardens" and would look out back to see a bunch of concrete and a few blades of grass and was very confused at what they thought they were growing.

Lesson learned.

Watch Out for the Bushes!
Driving and Transportation in the UK

When I first moved to the UK as a student, I made sure that everyone around me, stranger or not, was well aware that I was NEVER going to drive in the UK. I could barely cross the road at that point without getting smushed to a pulp, let's be honest. Getting behind the wheel of a moving vehicle was absolutely not going to happen unless I was in the front seat of the DLR (a London train) pretending to drive it.

Of course, as you may have realized by now, the vast majority of expat life includes doing things way out of your comfort zone.

As it went, I decided to move in with Guy while doing my Master's Degree so we could both save money and maybe live somewhere nicer than a single room in a rundown house with six other people we didn't know. We had many conversations about our ideal location, and I was always quick to mention that I wanted to live within walking distance from a train station.

So obviously we moved into a quaint little flat in the middle of the woods, about a fifteen minute drive away from a train station. Walking or biking was out of the question and would have taken hours and probably involved getting attacked by wild animals or something.

It made sense at the time, and I was fully on board with living there. I loved the flat for what it was for us – a place to grow our relationship and call our own. It was the first place I've ever lived in the UK that I could really call "mine."

However, it forced me to learn how to drive in the UK, and my then-terrified expat self was not at all happy about it.

See, I learned how to drive in Florida, where we definitely do not even attempt parallel parking (a staple on the UK driving test.) My driving test at home involved "regular" parking straight on, going about thirty miles an hour at most on a backroad, and then stopping without launching the tester through the window.

The sheer thought of navigating roundabouts and box junctions and weird traffic patterns I had never heard about was enough to make me cry myself to sleep, but learning to do all that on the other side of the road? I was beside myself with fear.

Because I had been less than a year in the country on that visa, I was allowed to drive with my American license at first. You have a full year in the UK before you need to switch to a UK license.

I'm not even sure why they allow us to use our American licenses because let me tell you, that thing did not in any way qualify me to drive down a one way road built for a horse and cart on a foggy English morning.

Anyway, I had awhile until I had to actually take a test to get a new license, so the first thing to do was actually learn how to drive again.

The problem (one of many) was that most cars in UK are "stick shift," or what our ever so classy British counterparts would call a "manual transmission"

I had never learned how to drive stick shift in America – there was just no opportunity and no point, given that all of my family's cars were them automatic and most cars in the US are automatic as well. And if I was going to learn, I certainly wasn't up for doing it somewhere where I also had to drive on the other side of the road.

Guy pleaded with me to learn. "It's so much easier to find a car that has a manual transmission," he said. "You won't be able to drive my car if you don't learn. This is what everybody here does."

But I was stubborn in my refusal. A combination of sheer terror and the fact that I was felt expected to confirm to the British way all the time helped me dig my heels in and reaffirm that if I was going to drive in the UK, it was only going to be an automatic.

He finally gave in, mostly because I gave him no other choice and asserted that it was my driving experience and I was going to determine how it was done. I used classic expat phrases like, "I've already had to adjust to so much here" as an excuse for sticking to an automatic, and me driving at all was better than me not driving, so that was that.

Oh, and there may have also been an incident where he let me try to drive his car in the neighbourhood and I only got three houses down before panicking and giving up after clunking his car into some unnatural gear.

If you choose to learn how to drive stick shift or already know how, you will be qualified to take the full British driving license test, as opposed to the automatic-only one. This will, without a doubt, open you up to even more freedom in the UK as you would be able to drive any car. Don't be scared of learning based on my hesitation to do it. We all make different changes in the UK, some more, some less, and while this wasn't a change I was willing to make, it might fill you with a lot less fear and be something worth going for!

Once it had been decided that I was going to stick with automatic cars, we had to actually source an automatic car – they are available in the UK, but are outnumbered at dealerships and online auctions by manual cars. This gave us less choice, and throughout the years I've been driving in the UK, I've gone through a couple due to a fault with the first, but I've always managed to find one.

The Learning Process

"Oh my god, oh my god. I'm so nervous," I said as I was inching along the street, trying to wrap my head around both driving on the left side of the road while doing the actual steering from the right side of the car.

"You're doing fine. Just don't get so far to the left," Guy said, calmly, eyeing the shrubbery that was quickly approaching him.

"STOP SHOUTING AT ME!" I responded, my hands shaking.

"I'm not shouting at you. OH MY GOD, WHY ARE YOU DRIVING ME INTO A BUSH?" he screamed as I veered too far from the left.

"I CAN'T DO THIS!" I yelled back.

"PULL OVER, I'M DRIVING!" he shouted.

I stopped the car and starting crying while telling him all about how I was going to move back to America and I was done here.

There are many things that your partner can teach you how to do. Make their favorite recipe. File your taxes. Paint a wall.

But when it comes to driving, I quickly learned that having your English boyfriend teach you was actually worse than when your mom would take you out on the road at 16 and she would spend the whole time grabbing onto the center console and gasping erratically acting like you were going straight for the neighbor's mailbox.

Now, don't get me wrong – Guy was very helpful in teaching me how to drive in England in many ways, but it became apparent that my fear and his inability to understand why I was so scared (and also resentful of the fact I had to change "my" way of doing things) led to a not-so-fantastic learning environment.

While he did take me out on the road for the beginning lessons, which did eventually improve from the first one, I also started practicing on my own and hired a driving instructor to give me some lessons.

Taking driving lessons is actually incredibly common in the UK. In the US, many of us just learn from friends and family members and then take the test, but the UK test is much more involved than the driving test in many States and the rules of the road are perhaps a bit more complicated given the smaller roads and roundabouts. Just ask in your local area for some driving instructor or driving school recommendations and people will be able to provide you with the names of some of the best.

I took two, two-hour driving lessons to give me the best chance to get a license as a foreigner in the UK. Other people take many more – it's up to you.

My instructor came and picked me up in his car for the first lesson, and then for the second, once he was confident that I knew how to drive well, he let me have the final lesson in my own car as I prepared for the test.

Having that driving instructor was invaluable because it was a much calmer learning process, and he knew the test back to front.

He knew which maneuvers to teach me, tricks for getting them done well (parallel parking, I'm looking at you!) and what kind of questions they might ask me to start off the test.

Seriously, don't be embarrassed to take driving lessons.

In fact, it will probably save you money in the long run as you'll have a much better chance of passing the first time instead of having to pay the test fee over and over again until you finally will yourself through it.

Another thing I did that I found helpful when I was learning to drive was to really watch what my boyfriend was doing when he was driving, and asking him questions along the way.

Once I started to know the answers about why he would stop in a certain place or park in a certain way or give way to a certain car, I would then explain his driving as he was driving.

So, for instance, "You slowed down there because you always yield to the right on a roundabout," and he would confirm (or deny!) that what I said was correct.

This only works, I suppose, if you are with someone who is actually good at driving in the UK and not just crazily speeding through traffic lights, so do be cautious!

Differences in Driving in the UK and US

Part of the adjustment process in learning to drive in the UK is due to switching to driving on the left side of the road, but to be honest I think it's the other rules and regulations that are harder to get nailed down in your head!

This isn't a driving manual – for the rules of the road, you'll need to study up on the UK Highway Code. But here are some of the main sticking points that many Americans won't be used to.

Roundabouts

A roundabout, also known as a traffic circle in some parts of the world, is a replacement for an intersection. Instead of all cars needing to stop and go when their light is the right color, the traffic keeps flowing and when you go is based on when you have no one coming on your right hand side.

Roundabouts aren't often single lanes, though – there are usually multiple lanes and different signals (or indicators as they're called in the UK) you need to give depending on when you're ready to leave the roundabout onto the road again.

To give you an idea of how much experience I had with roundabouts before moving to the UK, they once built a roundabout in a shopping center in my hometown. We were all perplexed, but excited to feel a bit European and figure out how to use this new traffic pattern.

Unfortunately, we didn't get to practice for long because they removed it due to the number of people who didn't realize they needed to do the "round" part of a "roundabout" and instead just drove straight through the middle.

Brits are shocked at our lack of roundabouts in the US – they view them as the best option for keeping traffic flowing and my husband dies a thousand culture shock deaths when we have to wait for a long time at a light in the US!

Of course, once you've conquered the rules of a single roundabout, you can then get used to a double roundabout where you come off one roundabout straight into another. If you really feel like testing your skills or crying a lot, you can try the Magic Roundabout in Swindon, which is seven roundabouts in one. Yes, you heard me right.

Traffic Lights

The only thing I have to mention about traffic lights is that, firstly, most are standing up in a vertical fashion rather than hanging from above you. And secondly, they go from green to yellow to red like American ones, but then also go from red to yellow to green! I love this, as it shows both the cars when their turn is almost here, as well as pedestrians that they need to get the heck out of the road (or they should be by that point anyway!)

Pedestrian Crossings

Speaking of pedestrians, the UK is much more pedestrian-friendly than most of the US, and there are multiple different types of pedestrian crossings.

Many have animal names like "zebra" and "pelican" just to make it that much more fun.

In general, expect to yield to pedestrians in the UK and be much more aware of people on foot. Brits will walk just about anywhere, as evidenced by the story that my sister-in-law tells about the time she was in Texas and decided to walk along a major road with no sidewalk and wondered why everyone was staring at her!

Street and Road Signs

Because the UK runs on roundabouts, you won't find the same layout of road signs like stop signs everywhere because there are not usually intersections to stop at! Instead, you'll see a lot of "yield" signs and other road signs that help a driver know who has the right of way. Learning the UK road signs is an essential part of studying for your theory test.

You'll also soon see that the actual street signs are not held up by a tall separate pole in the ground, but often attached to the buildings themselves in busy cities. In the suburbs, you might find them as a separate structure, but it will be much lower to the ground so if you don't see the road name, look down!

Box Junctions

A "box junction" is a junction which is filled with diagonal lines that indicates that you need to leave the junction (or intersection) clear. You are expected to wait at the "start" of the box until you can make sure that you have enough room on the other side to clear it.

Small Country Lanes

The UK was not made for cars. On the contrary, the roads were made first, mostly to fit horses, and cars came along way later.

This means that the roads are smaller, and also that there are tons of narrow country lanes that can barely fit me after a large meal, much less my car. Or at least, that's how I see it. My husband has no problem driving them confidently and assures me he has "plenty of space" while I'm literally two inches away from the hedges.

The thing about these lanes is that they are often only big enough for one car to fit through, so you will find yourself needing to judge the traffic ahead and finding places to pull over and let someone pass.

This is a huge difference for me, coming from Florida, where all of our roads are wide enough for someone's monster truck.

Often, there will also be roads that are not necessarily small country lanes, but "regular roads" with no median. The lanes might be marked, or might not, but you're expected to just stay on your side and know the rules of the road. I'm still not used to feeling that close to other cars whizzing past me going the opposite direction, but mention it to a Brit and they'll mostly have no inclination that it can or should be any other way!

Obstacles Everywhere

If you're used to driving in city areas, you may already be used to dodging obstacles everywhere you go, but driving in the UK seemed to be filled with more hazards on the road than I was used to.

Not everyone has driveways (called simply "drives" here), and that means that many people are parking on the road, even if they live on a main thoroughfare where people drive quite fast! You also have a favorite British pastime, the weekend cyclers or bicyclists who especially come out in force in good weather. And in more rural areas, it's not unusual to come past a tractor or some horses also sharing the road with you.

Being aware of your surroundings is always a necessity when being behind a wheel, but especially in the UK, I've learned to anticipate and react to things in my path.

That is, of course, until I ran my car straight into a parked van because I was temporarily blinded by the sun and it was parked in the road, but we won't talk about that.

Parking

Every time my husband comes to the US, he's known to point out parking spaces, only for us to be like "no! I'll never fit in there!"

"Of course you can!" he'll say, and we'll still drive by it because we don't have the clearance we want.

His "you can squeeze into that parking spot" attitude comes from his experience growing up in the UK, where parking spaces and cars tend to be much smaller. Sometimes I'll feel like I need to hold my breath when he's parking about six inches away from other cars, but he always makes it just fine because he's British and I think that means you're just born good at fitting into small spaces.

As I mentioned before, in Florida we have so much room and parking options that we really don't learn how to parallel park. Maybe there are a few places where you could do it, but a lot of us aren't proficient at it and will happily park miles away to not have to do it.

Compare that to the UK, where parallel parking could very well come up on your test and many parking spots in places around the country are only parallel parking on the street. I spent hours learning how to parallel park when I was studying for my driving test and eventually got the hang of it, though I'll still never get used to not having feet of clearance on other side of me when I'm parking.

That leads me to another point – if you're from suburban or rural America, you may be shocked at how limited parking can seem in the UK. Again, everything is smaller, and so parking is at a premium. "Where can I park?" is a question often asked by many people making appointments, buying tickets for a show or just generally wanting to go shopping in town.

Parking is also often paid for with time limits more often than in America. Not just metered parking, but parking lots (known as "car parks" in the UK) where you will have a two or three hour time limit or need to pay and them get reimbursed when you buy something from the store.

Even most hospitals have paid-for parking, which some think is unfair due to the vulnerable nature of people who need hospital appointments or need to visit people at the hospital, but the rationale is that if it were free parking, people who didn't need those spaces and simply wanted parking to get themselves somewhere else close by would use them up.

Even outside houses, people get funny about their parking spots. We have a parking spot for our house that is actually a bit of a drive away, but there are also public spaces in front of our row of terraced houses. When we first moved in, my husband parked in one of them, only to come out and find later than someone had parked directly behind him in an effort to block him in and make a point.

It turned out later that this person believed the parking spot to be "his," despite the fact that it was officially on the land registry documents as a public space. Finding parking in our neighbourhood can be a challenge, which forces many people to park on the street or not next to their house, and he wasn't willing to concede that this parking spot wasn't actually "his."

I convinced Guy to stop parking there because it wasn't worth a feud with a neighbor, but every time we pull in, he always looks at the space, if unoccupied, and complains about not being able to park there.

If you haven't caught on already, parking can be a contentious issue across the UK!

Practical Tips for Getting a License in the UK

Now that we've talked about some of the things that UK drivers go through and you have gotten a glimpse into my own very perilous experience learning to drive here, I wanted to give you some practical tips to help you figure out the process of applying for and getting a license in the UK if that's on your expat horizon.

Apply for your provisional (learner's) license after 6 months of living in the UK (the minimum amount of time you need to wait)

When you send off for your provisional license, you must send off your passport to the DVLA, the equivalent to the DMV. This is also terrifying, but you have no other choice so just do it.

Mine came back pretty quickly, but always best to be prepared as you can't book any of your tests without it.

This also means that you shouldn't plan to apply for your provisional license at the same time that you need your passport for visa purposes, for travel, or for other identification where it would be a bad situation to not have it with you.

You must get the provisional license before you take your driving test, but if you have an American license and are within a year of moving to the UK, you can still drive by yourself and not need someone with you. If you didn't have an American license, it would essentially be like having your learning permit in America where someone needs to be with you while driving at all times.

Study Hard for your Theory Test

Before you take any sort of road test, you have to pass the theory test. This is taken in test centers across the UK, and your nearest one will be revealed to you when you're ready to book.

This is a sit-down exam where you sit at a computer and do both multiple choice questions and a hazard perception test. The multiple choice questions are self-explanatory, and you can study for them using the many handbooks available.

The hazard perception test involves you watching clips of someone driving, as if you're behind the wheel, and you have to "click" to indicate potential hazards. Again, there are plenty of study tools available to help you understand how to "click accurately."

The theory test is just the first of the two tests you must take, the second being the practical one, so I would advise to study as much as possible to pass this on the first go so you're not holding yourself up getting to the actual driving test.

Book your driving test as far away from a main city as possible

You can take your UK practical driving test at any center in the UK, and some of them have MUCH higher pass rates than others.

There are websites that will show you the pass rates, and while you shouldn't use that as a crutch, it's obviously going to be a more difficult test in busier conditions or closer to a city.

We live outside of London, and I made sure to take mine further away from London rather than in it or anywhere near it.

In fact, there is a pretty large town near us that many people take their driving tests in, and I still didn't want to do that as I felt it was too busy and congested and would freak me out.

So instead, I went to a smaller town with more open space and more room on the roads.

I also scheduled it for a weekday when people would be at work or otherwise at home, not doing the school run or rushing home from a long day at the office.

Some remote areas in Scotland have over 70% pass rates because you don't really have any 'hazards' besides a sheep or two, so if you're really struggling, there's always that option!

Learn the Driving Test in Advance

The UK driving test is much more intense than what I experienced in the US. It's not just a quick jaunt around a parking lot, but a driving test on main roads and around a city (not on highways, but everywhere else). Mine took about 45 minutes, and in addition to driving around the local area, you will be expected to answer some verbal questions about how your car works, potentially show that you know things about how to operate your car's lights, wipers, and other less-used features, and perform some parking and maneuvers.

Even if you have driven in the US for years, you still need to make sure you are prepared for the UK test and familiarize yourself with it in advance. This is part of what getting a driving instructor is good for, but you can also research a lot online and watch YouTube video tutorials about what to expect.

The more you go in knowing what's about to happen and what will be expected of you, the more confident you can be.

In the end, I think the driving examiner took it easy on me after hearing that I had driven in the US for years, as one of her "do you know your car?" questions was asking me to demonstrate I could honk the horn. I passed that one with flying colors, if you're wondering.

You should also learn the way the test is graded – there are "minor" mistakes that you can make and still pass up to a certain amount, as well as "major" mistakes that will earn you an automatic fail.

Knowledge is power in this instance, and if for some reason you don't pass on the first try, don't fret – it's common to not pass on the first try and you just have to keep doing it until that UK license is in your hands!

Enjoy your freedom

I was so scared to learn to drive in the UK for years, and after I finally was forced into it, I am so glad I did.

Especially as an expat, you find that sometimes you feel as if you are dependent on everyone else to help you get by or guide you and it can lead to a feeling of being "stuck" or helpless. As soon as I learned to drive, the town that we lived in became "mine" and I began to explore and branch out a bit more. Even having the freedom to go to the grocery store on my own and go shopping was huge.

The culture shock that you experience as an expat can be hard to overcome until you feel like you really belong and have the same opportunities and abilities as people who live in the country. Getting your driver's license in the UK as a foreigner is an important way to do that.

I also think the sooner you learn to do it, the better. Don't give yourself time to build up nerves about it or get so worked up in your head about feeling stuck. The longer you wait, the scarier it will seem. Take each step of the process slowly, but with confidence. Do your research, and just book it!

Trust me, if I in my infinite panic could do it, there's no reason you can't!

Car Insurance for Expats

When you're searching for car insurance in the UK as a foreign driver, make sure to do a search for "best insurance for expats" or "foreign drivers" rather than just UK car insurance. I always use one of the comparison tools to find the best prices, as unfortunately car insurance for expats is going to be quite high in the beginning.

This is because, even if you've driven for 100 years, you will only be a "new" UK driver. In fact, when I actually passed my driving test and was insured on a UK license rather than an American one, the "years of driving" I was allowed to put down decreased because they then counted my years on a

UK license rather than just any license.

Public Transportation in the UK

Whether you're headed to London or Birmingham or Manchester or Edinburgh or one of the other awesome UK cities, you might be looking at all of this and wondering if you even need a car. If it's London you're living in, you definitely won't need one, for instance, as the entire city runs on public transportation like the tube and buses.

For other locations, chat to some locals first to see what they do. You may be surprised to find out that everyone just takes the local buses or uses their own two feet.

Public transportation is alive and well across the UK, and even in what I would deem "rural" areas, there will often be some type of regular bus to help people get where they are going. There are also trams, subway systems, river boats and other ways of getting around without needing a car in many towns and cities.

Another positive shock to the American expat system in the UK is the ease of taking trains and buses all around the country. The train network is vast and well-connected, and many people base their living situations off of the nearest train station. Whether for commuting purposes or just having a "weekend away," Brits are constantly on trains and public transportation.

I'm from the suburbs of Orlando, which is not exactly the capital of public transportation and is very much an area where you need a car if you want to have any sort of life. My husband is always shocked by this every time he visits and finds it odd that we seem to spend all of our time going from building to building in our cars. He also just about keels over with laughter every time we go through a bank or ATM or pharmacy drive thru – they're not common, if at all existent, in the UK, so get ready to park and get out of your car!

Be Confident in What You Need

Health in the UK and Navigating the NHS

A few years ago, I sat patiently in the waiting room of an NHS (National Health Service) dermatologist after having been referred by my GP (general practitioner - more on that later).

I was there because my acne hadn't cleared up, even in my 20s, and I had remembered that my American dermatologist as a teenager had recommended that I go on a very strong and serious drug, Acccutane.

Luckily for me, I thought I had learned the ways of the NHS beforehand and knew immediately when I went to my GP that I needed to just come straight out with what I wanted (to be referred to a dermatologist) and be firm in my stance.

My GP is an incredibly friendly and easygoing guy, so he asked me a few question about my history with acne and then "referred" me on, which meant the dermatologist in my area got in touch with me to schedule an appointment a few weeks later.

By the time I was called into the consultant's room at the dermatologist's office, I felt like I was pretty much set. All I would have to do is tell them that I want to go on Accutane and I would walk out with the prescription.

"How can I help today?" asked the rather bored sounding dermatologist. She was friendly, but I clearly did not have any rashes or weirdly large moles she needed to deal with. I just had acne.

"I've dealt with acne since I was in middle school, and it hasn't cleared up yet," I said confidently. "My previous dermatologist recommended Accutane, and I'd like to try it."

If you've had any experience with the NHS yet yourself, you'll probably be laughing at me right now, but I genuinely believed that if I just walked in and requested it, that's what I would get.

Perhaps this was brought about by my experience with the American healthcare system, where doctors would often try and put me on drugs and treatments for my acne that I wasn't even entirely sure I wanted to do. I had come from a world where we choose our own doctors, and if one doesn't give you what you want, you simply move on to the next. Whether or not this American healthcare system culture is dangerous is a topic for another book, but there's no denying that it's different.

She looked at me quizzically and proceeded to stare at my face for a few seconds.

"I don't think your acne is bad enough for Accutane," she said matter-of-factly. "I can prescribe you some topical treatments."

I felt like I had been punched in the gut.

"I've tried topical treatments," I said, pulling out a list of medications I had been on over the years. I showed them to her, putting the paper in front of her face desperately.

She read the list and looked at my skin again.

"I really don't think that it's bad enough to warrant Accutane," she repeated.

I stared at her, getting more and more emotional at the thought of going on another treatment that was only meant to calm my acne for the short term, and almost never worked.

"I have had acne since I was 11," I said, starting to cry. "I have tried tons of treatments and nothing has worked permanently. I am over 20 years old now, and I'm tired of it. My dermatologist in the UK has been recommending Accutane for years. Please can I go on Accutane."

In that moment she seemed to understand that she was dealing with an American who wasn't going to give up what she wanted, or maybe she just needed to get on to the next appointment and couldn't be bothered.

"Okay," she said. "You can go on Accutane, provided you go to all of the follow up appointments and pass the initial blood test."

I was relieved, but felt annoyed that I needed to "fight" for my case. I felt at a disadvantage, not having UK medical records and not having that same sort of relationship as I would have with my American dermatologist that I had seen for the past five or so years.

If you're wondering, I went on to pass the blood tests and do the full course of Accutane. This is not a recommendation for the drug, but in my personal experience it cleared up my skin beautifully, and in the following years I haven't regretted pushing for what treatment I wanted.

After this experience, I gained a better understanding of how the medical system in the UK works and why I have to always go in prepared to ask for what I want and to accept that it's not the same as it is in the US.

It makes sense, of course, that the NHS plays a more conservative, "wait and see" approach to many ailments. Firstly, when you pay through healthcare through your taxes rather than privately, there is more onus on the NHS to get it right and not spend needlessly. Every single person who has ever had a pimple can't go in demanding an expensive and dangerous treatment – in my case she gave in because I had my past medical records to back it up and showed her how this acne was affecting me emotionally.

Compare that to the US where I've had friends who have gone on Accutane that only ever had mild acne that was just annoying rather than emotionally (or physically) scarring. Doctors seem more ready to prescribe treatments in the US because you're going to be on the hook for a lot of that cost. If you're willing to pay, then you're likely to be able to find someone willing to let you proceed.

In some ways, these different systems have shown me just how much the American healthcare system is driven by pharmaceutical companies. You would never see a commercial (called an advert) in the UK for a drug, encouraging you to ask your doctor to prescribe it to you. Instead, you go to the doctor, tell them your symptoms, they'll run tests if needed, and then they prescribe you the medication that they think will work best for you.

To me, this method is highly preferable to getting attached to medications because you saw a family on the television having a lovely breakfast around the table with the sun shining through the window and you want to look as happy as the actor that plays the mother.

However, there are downsides to the NHS too that some expats run into when comparing the systems. In addition to their more conservative approach towards treatment or getting scans, there is also usually a slower wait time when it comes to being referred on to other doctors and specialists, unless they suspect it is urgent in which case they will get you in as fast as possible. You also need to go through your GP first to be referred onto many other specialists, so it's not as simple as making an appointment with your own dermatologist or orthopaedic surgeon or a gynaecologist if you're using the NHS.

NHS Basics

To help you wrap your head around the NHS terminology and history if you haven't been in the UK for a while, let's take a moment to break down some of what you might hear and how you need to navigate it.

NHS Terminology

NHS: the National Health Service, founded in 1948 under the ideal that good healthcare should be available to all.

GP: General Practitioner, the main doctor that you see based on the area you live in.

A&E: Accident and Emergency, the same thing as an Emergency Room

Referral: when your GP refers you on to a specialist doctor.

Surgery: this means the doctor's office, as in "the doctor's surgery." The word "surgery" is also used if you're actually getting surgery, so you have to use context clues to figure out which one to say in the moment!

How to Use the NHS

When You Have an Issue to Talk to a Doctor About

Let's say, like me, you wanted to talk to a doctor about your acne or something that you know can definitely wait for an appointment. In this case, you need to first make sure you're registered with your local doctor. This is done by area and you do not have a choice many times if you're using the NHS.

Once registered, you need to go through their appointment system, whether this means calling the morning of for an appointment that same-day or using their system to book ahead of time if possible.

You will then speak to a doctor at the surgery during your appointment, which are slotted to be ten minutes long. If you have multiple issues, you are encouraged to tell the receptionist this when making an appointment as you are really supposed to stick to your scheduled time.

If the doctor has a solution for your problem or has medication to prescribe you, that's it – you might make a follow-up appointment with them or need to go to the pharmacy to collect your medication, but you're all done!

If, on the other hand, they feel the need to refer you on to a specialist, they will either print out a referral letter that lets you make an appointment with your area's specialist in that area, or it will be electronic and that department will contact you to make an appointment.

Sometimes, the appointment may be weeks or months away depending on how urgent the problem is. If cancer is suspected, you will be fast tracked and there is a rule that you shouldn't have to wait more than two weeks for a specialist appointment.

It's also important to know that pharmacists in the UK are often legally able to prescribe you medications based on your symptoms if you believe you have some sort of flu, infection, cold, burn, etc. They are not just simply there to dispense the medication, so don't be afraid to start your questioning with a pharmacist as you won't need an appointment and they can at least help get you on the right track of who you should be seen by.

When You Have an Issue You're Not Sure is an Emergency

If you have an issue and you're not sure if you need to get checked out right away or not, there is a telephone system called 111 where you call and speak to someone who will advise you on the next step to take based on your symptoms.

Many hospitals also have "urgent care" areas or "minor injuries unit," which are not to be confused with what an American would think of as an "urgent care center," but it is somewhere where you could go with injuries that are a step down from true "emergency" but still need to be seen sooner rather than later.

When You Have an Emergency

If you have an emergency of any type, you should get yourself to the closest Accident and Emergency room or call the emergency number – 999. It's a good idea to have this written down somewhere, as it sounds silly, but when I had been living in the UK for about two to three years, I got into a car accident and needed to call the police.

Because I was so shaken up, I kept dialing 911 and suddenly "999" slipped right out of my mind – we are ingrained with habits that are hard to break, and often in trauma your mind might go right back to 911.

However you get yourself to the hospital, you will then be seen, triaged, and treated. If you need to be admitted to the hospital, you will be. Once you've been discharged, you will be told to make an appointment with your GP to follow up.

When You Want Regular Scans and Tests

There are some scans and tests, like mammograms, that many American women are used to getting regularly in the US. The guidance on how often you should get regular screenings are sometimes different than in the US, and you may feel as though you are getting prompted to get screened less than you would in the States and at a later age.

For example, cervical screening for women on the NHS is every three years from the age of 25, whereas the American Cancer Society recommends starting at age 21, but then going to every five years from the age of 30.

If you have any worrying symptoms, you will be sent for any scans the doctor thinks is necessary no matter when you had your last screenings, but if you are wanting more frequent screenings for any part of your body than the NHS recommends, you can consider going to a private healthcare provider for that (which I'll touch on in a bit).

Costs on the NHS

As Americans used to worrying about the cost every time we go to the doctor's office and thinking about things like "in-network," you should know that it's entirely different in the UK.

As an expat here, you would have likely paid some sort of NHS fee upon applying for your visa. This entitles you to register at a doctor's surgery and get free treatment on the NHS for many conditions. It doesn't cost money when you go to the doctor's or specialists or emergency room, and your only cost would usually be prescriptions.

Also, if you're used to the cost of American prescriptions, you might be delighted to hear that prescriptions cost a standardized amount in England – around £9 per prescription. That's right. £9. So that course of Accutane I was on that would have cost hundreds of dollars in the States? Just £9 for my monthly doses.

If you're in Wales, Northern Ireland, or Scotland, prescriptions on the NHS are free of charge regardless of who you are, and prescriptions are also free in England to those with various circumstances like ongoing disability, low income, and other things.

If you're in the UK and aren't on a visa yet, you can still get treatment. Emergency treatment is free for all, and if you need other treatment, you can pay (still cheaper prices than going without insurance in the US) and get seen.

Things to Keep in Mind about the NHS

Sometimes, navigating the NHS can be confusing and stressful for an

American used to having more control over our health care. We hear lots of fearmongering in the US regarding nationalized health services, and fear that we won't get the same quality of care in the UK as we would in the US.

In my experience, while the doctor's offices and hospitals in the UK are nowhere near as "flashy" and pristine as in the US, the actual care that you receive here is not necessarily worse or better than in the US. The UK has some brilliant doctors, and if something urgent is suspected, like cancer, they will make sure to prioritize you in the system and get you seen as fast as possible.

When I feel a bit stressed about adjusting to the different systems, I like to remind myself of the one benefit of the NHS that cannot be overlooked: you never fear in the UK that your family is going to have to go broke if someone gets a life-threatening illness. I do not debate whether I can afford to the doctor's office – I go MORE here than I ever did in the US because I go when I have a medical issue, not when I have enough leftover from a paycheck to cover my co-pay.

The other thing to note is that you do not have to use the NHS. You can always opt for private medical attention in the UK. This allows you to pay more (sometimes a lot more) in exchange for being seen faster, usually. However, keep in mind that the system really is NHS dominated and private practices are much rarer. There has been some controversy surrounding whether private practices are upholding the same standards as the NHS, but you can always look into private practices near you if you feel you need other options for your care.

For those of us who embrace and use the NHS (which is the majority of American expats), here are some things I've learned to help your visits go smoothly.

Pre-existing Conditions

If you have a pre-existing condition diagnosed in the States or you have any paperwork related to your condition or past treatments, make sure to keep this with you and bring to your appointment. Having some history on you will help the doctor make the appropriate decisions faster. In my case, being able to show that I had used topical treatments for my acne in the past helped the dermatologist to be able to check this off on her sheet that then allowed me to qualify for Accutane.

Advocate for Yourself

Be prepared to advocate for yourself in any doctor's room you walk into. You may not see the same doctor every time, which is a real adjustment for how we pick our doctors in the States. They could only know you from a file. To help them help you, be very clear about what your symptoms are and what you're hoping the outcome will be with your care.

For instance, if your back has been hurting for awhile and you've already taken ibuprofen, go in prepared to tell them that you want to be referred for physiotherapy or for scans to diagnose the problem. Sometimes, because of the "wait and see" approach, they might want to first suggest you try some stronger pain killers for issues like that instead of getting down to the root of the problem right away.

Convey Emotions

Make it clear how your problem is affecting your daily life, if it is. For example, my acne was affecting my self-esteem and mental well-being, and mentioning that helped the dermatologist understand how severe this problem was for me. The NHS will often not cover conditions that are "cosmetic" or not actually harming you, but they will take your emotional well-being into account in many cases. They are not mind readers, so be clear with them how you are being affected by your condition!

Be Polite, but Firm

Be articulate about what is wrong with you and who you're hoping to be referred to, but also be polite. NHS doctors can be incredibly overworked, and being kind to them rather than being overbearing has done me a world of good. Stick up for yourself, but don't be rude. Learn how to ask for what you want and get answers to your questions without going in like a bull in an American healthcare china shop who wants to run over your doctor for merely suggesting that you do some exercises for your knee before they have you do the full head-to-toe scan with 26 types of dye.

British Attitudes towards Medical Care

"Was it the right choice to come in?" my husband asked the A & E doctor. He had been having intense stomach pain for two days, and despite the fact that it was abnormal for him and going on for two days, it took me about an hour of convincing and shouting, "IT IS FREE! WHY WON'T YOU GO TO THE EMERGENCY ROOM?"

The doctor gave a non-committal reply that neither confirmed nor denied that he had done the right thing in coming in, and I rolled my eyes at him on the way home as he questioned whether it was "okay" that he went.

I would have found this a very odd attitude towards going into A & E, if it weren't for the fact that a couple months prior I had an experience where someone was very, very sick in bed to the point that they were incoherent, and the people around this person debated for about 20 minutes between themselves whether they should call 999! And not because they didn't want to get this sick person help, but because they were justifying to themselves that it was "bad enough" to warrant inconveniencing anyone! Their leg could have been chopped off and they'd probably mutter a, "Oh dear, that's not good" and check the time to make sure they're not heading into A & E on anyone's lunch hour.

This very British approach to getting medical help seems to seep into going to the regular doctor's office as well – people aren't running to the doctor with every ache and pain usually. I pay no attention to this "wait and see" approach and show up at the doctor's office and A & E whenever I feel I need medical attention with no concern about inconveniencing the doctor, which is probably a sign that I have not fully transitioned into British life!

Mental Health

In recent years, headlines have focused on the failings of mental health services in the UK to adequately address the growing number of people coming forward with mental health concerns, but there is also evidence to suggest that this problem is slowly getting better.

In the UK, patients can get free mental health treatment on the NHS, but only after being referred and oftentimes being on a waiting list. Not all of this is in-person talk therapy, either. Someone I know has received mental health care on the NHS, but instead of talk therapy in-person, was provided with some forms to first fill out and then was offered a phone call with a therapist.

Of course, in the UK you can still go out of the NHS to access mental health services, and this is what many people do. From charities to private practitioners, you can schedule your own therapy and get seen more quickly – if you're willing to pay.

I'm not suggesting that I have the ultimate word on whether mental health services in the UK are better or worse than in the US. While the US might not suffer with waiting lists the same way the UK does, the prices for mental health help are often higher and may, in its own way, prevent people from getting the support they need.

If you struggle with stress, anxiety, or depression, you can actually refer yourself on the NHS. Otherwise, you should make an appointment with your GP, who can then either prescribe you medications, refer you for counseling, or refer you to a psychiatrist who can prescribe a wider array of mental health treatments.

Eye Care

For eye care in the UK, you will go to an optician directly. You can make your own appointment, and they will do an eye test and tell you where to get your glasses.

The NHS does provide some vouchers for free eye tests to certain people in various age groups or with various conditions, so check on that before you book one. Otherwise, the tests are not expensive – we usually pay about £20 per eye test.

Glasses, of course, are an additional cost, but this is the same as in the US.

Dentistry

I'm just going to throw it out there – one of the stereotypes of British people is that they have bad teeth. You can confirm or deny that for yourself, but I will say that British dentists focus more on the health of your teeth rather than the cosmetic look. This is, perhaps, where this stereotype has come from.

You do need to pay for your dentistry, but you can register as an NHS patient at some dentists and get discounted rates (there is sometimes a waiting list), or you can choose your own and go private.

Even private dentistry costs here are less than American dentistry costs, so fear not!

One of the main things to be aware of, here, if you are particularly into how white your teeth are and how they look, is to look for a US style dentist based on recommendations from fellow expats and to ensure that you have booked a cleaning in addition to a dental check-up, as it's not always combined into one.

In fact, this is one area where the general consensus among many American expats discussing dentistry is to go private from the start. Dental care on the NHS is focused on fixing issues or dental emergencies, not preventative dentistry like we are used to in America. It's fantastic if you do have a problem that you need fixed without sacrificing your next year's mortgage, but not so great when it comes to maintaining those pearly whites.

And similar to the doctor's offices, don't expect the dentist's office to look quite as flashy as you might be used to. Brits are shocked when I explain that my American dentist's office was designed to look like a living room with plush couches and a television in the waiting room and then flat screen televisions in every individual room so you can catch up on the latest HGTV remodel while getting your teeth cleaned.

Common Changes in Your Health and Body after Moving

When I first moved to the UK, I was sick a LOT. From a cold one week to a sore throat the next to weird aches and pains, I attributed it to my body adjusting to a new climate and the new bacteria and germs of a new country. This is a common occurrence for many expats, which is not to say to not get yourself checked out if you're worried about your health, but rather that you are not alone if your body feels just a little bit different after moving to the UK.

If you come from a different climate, you might also notice the dry skin that happens in the UK during the winter months especially! Being from Florida, which is never lacking in humidity, I wasn't prepared for my skin to feel so painful in the winter and quickly learned the wonderful ways of gloves and moisturizers to prevent them from drying out.

It's also really likely that you'll find your hair reacts differently to the water in the UK than at home. The water in much of the UK is very hard water, which means it has a high amount of dissolved minerals. Hard water can leave your hair feeling a bit dull and you may need to mix up your hair care routine or get a water softener if you find that your hair suddenly doesn't feel as healthy.

Work Hard, but Not Too Hard
Working Life in the UK

Since moving to the UK, I've been lucky enough to be employed in many different sectors.

Initially, as a study abroad student, I worked as a nanny for a very wealthy French family who lived in Kensington. This gave me no insight into workplace culture in the UK, but did show me how the "other half" lived and I got to go to France with them on vacation, so – all was not lost.

I also interned, during another study abroad program, for QVC UK, which to date has been one of the highlights of my workplace experiences. This was a real corporate affair, with plush work areas, its own cafeteria, and a stunning location in an office park that made me feel 18 different types of accomplished before I even stepped foot in the door. Here, I had a small team of coworkers who went out of their way to make me feel included and accepted, including helping me celebrate Thanksgiving and making me a giant

"Happy Thanksgiving" sign featuring printed off pictures of people and places they deemed quintessentially American.

After graduating, I worked as an intern at a (then) start-up company that delivered boxes of ingredients to your door so you could cook pre-portioned meals in the comfort of your home without having to worry about going to the store or purchasing exotic spices or ingredients in larger quantities than you needed.

Here, I worked with people from a wide variety of backgrounds, including many Europeans, and I got an up close look at the drama of start-up culture. There was less of a focus on my American-ness here, due to the hectic nature of the work day and the diversity of the existing teams. I didn't stand out among my coworkers by being from somewhere else, but I did stand out when I answered the phones with my American accent.

In fact, I panicked multiple times a day in the beginning when I would pick up the phone and hear a strong accent on the other line (particularly the Scottish ones I couldn't understand if my life depended on it). Sometimes I'd have to pretend that the line was breaking up so I could hang up on them and they could call back and speak to one of my colleagues who had a better ear for accents. I also had to learn how to read, write, and speak in British English, as I was responsible for answering e-mails in British English and I needed to use the correct words for food in the UK while speaking on the phone (for example, talking about their missing aubergine rather than eggplant).

After that, I got a job working within a government-funded organization. Not exactly working in the Houses of Parliament, but I was in an office in Westminster not too far away. The organization was focused on planning (the building and development kind, not the party kind), and I came in having absolutely no clue what a "council" was, much less the British attitudes towards developments (they usually hate new developments with little exceptions).

I had to learn the ins and outs of some pretty heavy and pretty boring terminology in order to effectively work in a Communications role with them, and while it was a great experience and fascinating to get to see the inner-workings of parts of the government, it was also a real challenge for me when it came to workplace culture.

For starters, we "hot desked," which is popular in the UK and made it so I never knew exactly where I would sit on any given day. We had lockers to store our belongings in, and every day you would come in and get your stuff out of your locker and then try and find an open seat at a desk in the area we generally sat in.

Many of my coworkers were traveling and working outside of the office as their roles required them to give trainings and meet people from all different parts of the UK, so you were never actually sure who was going to be in the office when you were in.

This made it hard for me to feel like I was fitting into the office culture when I couldn't really establish the existing dynamics for a long time, and I didn't have a space in the office to call my own or bring my personality to.

The majority of this team were British, and all older than I was and in different stages of life, so I did stand out again both for my age and for being American. People were nice, but I was never able to fit in the way that I had hoped.

Finally, I found a job opening working with American students in the study abroad sector in London, which was a welcome change from the work I had done on tweeting about the "planning rules" and trying to convince Brits that it really was a good thing the green space next to their community was being bulldozed through.

The American study abroad sector in the UK is filled with both American expats and Brits who fell into study abroad through another route. I am the only American in my office of three, but here, being American is an asset rather than any sort of hindrance. To be able to understand our students on a deeper level and connect with them culturally both gives me an insight to be able to do my job better and make suggestions for how we run our programs, as well as makes me feel a bit more connected to what's going on in the States.

This is the smallest office I've ever worked in, but it is also the most fun. At this job, I feel relaxed, I feel happy to go in every morning (minus the soul-crushing commute which we'll talk about later) and I feel like I'm really contributing to a team and making a difference in the world in some small way.

I am still the "odd one out," in all of my American glory and spend about 80% of the time not understanding the anecdotes about their childhood television shows or other British culture references that my coworkers make, but it is something that I laugh rather than fret about.

I share my work history not to bore you to death, but to show you that I have worked in so many different types of offices and had lots of different experiences regarding workplace culture in the UK. When I talk about workplace culture in the UK, I know that it can't be generalized because every office and organization is truly different. Working at a charity shop in Cornwall is going to be different than working in a financial institution in London, and working for the government is going to be very different than working at a school.

However, along the way I've been able to pinpoint some of the main problems and questions that arise for American expats when figuring out how to get jobs in the UK, fit in to British workplace, and finally learn how to do the "tea rounds" once and for all.

How to Find a Job in the UK as an American Expat

One of the first hurdles is actually finding a job in the UK as an American expat. Often, expats are either here because they have married a Brit who already has a career set up, or they have moved with their American partner who has gotten a job in the UK and potentially have had to give up their own career back in the States.

If you are in the UK on a work visa yourself, then lucky you, you've accomplished this part so skip to the next!

It can be daunting to figure out how to land jobs in the UK when everything seems just slightly different. For instance, the American "resume" is the British "CV," which can be confusing because Americans associate a "CV" with something you would only use if you were an academic.

The basic idea behind an American resume and British CV are the same, except the British CV tends to have a bit more personal information about your interests and things you enjoy doing outside of the office.

Other differences to keep in mind are cultural understandings of what you've done in the past. For instance, sorority or fraternity experience isn't quite understood in the UK at best and highly judged at the worst.

You should also make sure that your British CV is in British English and uses British terminology. If you've been an "intern" in America, that's considered to be a "trainee" in the UK. If the internship was for class credit and not for pay, that would be closer to "work experience" in the UK.

It's also important to make sure, where necessary, that you explain your visa situation and living situation. If you have the right to work in the UK already, make that clear. Sometimes employers may see a history of American work experience and not want to go through the process of checking that you have the right to work.

Similarly, it's obviously best to apply from within the country as you can then use your British address on your CV and not even bring attention to your nationality. If you're applying from America with the plans of moving to the UK soon, then definitely clear this up as well so they know when you will be in the country and when you can start.

Some people manage to find jobs right away in the UK, while others go through a lot of trials and tribulations before finding something that suits them, but all you can do is to continue applying. Get someone you trust in the UK to look over your cover letters and CVs before sending to see if you're making any errors there, and make sure to stay professional in all interactions – you'll get there.

Sometimes the hurdles come from not having experience in a UK workplace, even if you've worked in your sector in the US for years, and in that case you could always try and do some volunteer work related to your sector in the UK while you search for a job to get something UK-based on your CV. You should also make sure that your qualifications transfer over and that any new courses or tests you need to take to be qualified to do your job in the UK are listed on your CV.

And if you have to – start small. You might not be able to immediately go into the same exact role you were in the US, but take what you can get to show your willingness to work and to get used to life in the UK, and then use that experience to work your way up and apply for new roles with the ability to discuss your UK experience.

Why You Should Work as an Expat

At certain points in my expat journey, I had work restrictions or wasn't allowed to work at all. This especially applies to many student visas, but it can also be the case if you're on a fiancé visa, for example.

As it turns out, those were some of my darkest times because I was bored out of my mind and felt like I was stuck in the house, peering out the window like the big bad wolf had locked me in there.

Sure, I could join hobby groups and get out and go to the store or head to the gym, but I felt like I didn't have a purpose. Working as an expat gave me a sense of belonging and somewhere to go where I was expected to show up at a certain time. It gave me routine and a schedule and something of my "own" outside of my relationship that I could cultivate and figure out for myself. Working gave me confidence and an insight into British culture that I could have only ever had in the workplace.

If there is any way that you can arrange your situation to have a job, even if it's a part-time one, I would highly encourage all American expats in the UK to do it. Even if you don't stick with it forever or if it's not your "calling," putting yourself out there in a work environment can be invaluable in making friends, learning more about the UK, and ultimately, even if it all falls apart, learning more about yourself and how you best adapt and adjust when you need to.

Making Friends at Work

Not all workplaces are designed to easily make friends, but I do think that coworkers can be an excellent source of friends in the UK or at least friendly acquaintances. It's worth putting in the effort to try and make friends in the office.

As we'll talk about in a minute, many workplaces in the UK thrive on a less intense work pace than that of America – it's not that less gets done, but more emphasis is put on small talk, drinking tea, and chatting before you get right down to business. This is the perfect opportunity to join in the office culture and be seen as relaxed and easygoing.

And that, as a matter of fact, is the main thing I've learned when it comes to making friends at work in the UK: do as they do.

This means saying "yes" to every invitation, whether it's to a social event after work or just to go around the corner with someone to the café to get lunch. Try your best to like drinking tea if you don't already, as saying "yes" to a cup of tea makes you seem like "one of them." When everyone is chatting when they get into the office, join in and see what kinds of questions they ask each other and what information they're sharing about themselves, their weekend or their opinions. Do the same (well, don't get all up in their personal space with your deepest darkest fears on your first day – actually, never do that).

And even when it goes against your positive American nature to join in on workplace complaining, don't underestimate the power of making friends through "moaning," as the British say. Complaining in the workplace is a way of bonding, whether it's about the work, the weather, public transportation on your way in or even the boss (eek!). Don't try and be the biggest complainer of them all, but feel free to vent a bit as well to connect with others.

Ultimately, just like as with other friendships, work friendships take time to cultivate and you can't speed up the process by anything other than being your friendly American self and getting involved.

Tea Culture

Tea when you first get in. Tea before lunch. Tea after lunch. Tea in the late afternoon. Tea before you leave.

Drinking tea is as omnipresent in many British workplaces as breathing. While Brits don't actually stop everything they're doing to enjoy a cup of tea at a specific time every day, many do drink it constantly throughout the work day and there is an entire culture devoted to tea and who makes it.

Here, making tea isn't just an "intern" thing or for the lowest person on the totem pole to do. Instead, when someone feels like making themselves a cup of tea, they'll usually ask around the office or to their team (depending on how big the office is) to see if anyone else wants one.

This means that you can feel like you're constantly being asked if you want tea, and while you have no obligation to say yes every time, it's a great way to "be one of them" and get in on office culture.

Then, later on in the day, it would be your unspoken "turn" to do the rounds and make the tea if you had accepted someone else making you a cup earlier. There is no rule that it is an even exchange, for example, if someone took you up on your offer, you don't have an obligation to take them up on their offer later, but the idea is that this continues into infinity so eventually, at the end of the universe, it will all even out.

I found it difficult at first to even know what I was doing in terms of making tea, as I didn't drink anything but iced tea back in the US and had never made a pot of British tea. This is a good skill to learn from a trusted British person when you first move to the UK so you can feel confident participating and knowing exactly what kinds of questions to ask people about how they like their tea.

Differences between Work in the US and UK

British Work Style

In *Watching the English*, Kate Fox has an entire section devoted to British workstyles, which I would highly recommend reading if you're about to enter the British workforce. In it, she talks all about many facets of life at work that really reflect British culture – for example, "moaning" or complaining to connect with others, not wanting to be seen as being too dedicated to your work without being lazy and the frequent small talk at the beginning of many work function and meetings.

In terms of British work styles, the biggest adjustment for me has been a more relaxed way of working. This is not to say that less gets done, but part of not wanting to appear too obsessed with your work involves doing things at a more leisurely pace and with a lack of the frenzy that surrounds many American workplaces. Americans tend to be known or thought of in the UK as having a frantic and demanding work environment, and that's just not the UK (or at least it's not the case for many workplaces here).

There are entire articles and research devoted to communication in the British workplace as well. "Can you do this when you get a chance?" may mean "I need this done right now," but the boss will communicate it in a convoluted vague and very British way that might go over the heads of a well-meaning American not used to that style of direction.

Overall, I've found that I take my cues in workplaces from others and I watch to observe how my colleagues react to things and the way they handle meetings and greetings so I can follow suit.

Time Off and Maternity Pay

One of the most noticeable differences between UK and American workplaces revolves around time off. The minimum amount of "holiday" or vacation time a full time British worker would receive is, including actual holidays, about five weeks!

To an American who may only usually get one or two weeks off per year, this seems absolutely crazy (in a good way, for many). Brits are astounded that American workers don't get the same amount of time off and there would be riots in the streets if ever you suggested the holiday allowance is decreased.

See what I mean about American workplaces being considered "frantic?"

I enjoy the extra time off here to the point that I genuinely couldn't see myself ever working a job in America again just due to the amount of freedom I would lose in many workplaces in terms of time off. You do have to request time off here – it still needs to fit within the needs of the company – but five weeks is five weeks!

Another area where the countries differ is in maternity pay. Brits have much better maternity pay laws than the US, and it is mandatory for an employee who has been with a company for at least six months to get fully paid maternity leave for two months and then up to a year at a pro-rated basis.

Salaries in the UK

When job hunting, you may find that the salaries in the UK are lower than that in the US. This isn't true for all sectors, but it is a hot topic of discussion in the expat community. You may be used to higher salary levels and have to take what appears, in your mind, as a pay cut when working in the UK.

Despite the initial shock of the numbers, it helps to try and take into account the other things the UK provides that the US doesn't. The cheaper healthcare, the better maternity pay, more vacation time and shorter working hours can all play a role in helping American expats in the UK to not get too concerned over the lower UK salary.

When job hunting in the UK, I would highly recommend researching the comparable salaries for your position in the UK rather than comparing to what you would have received in the US. Jobs in two different countries with two different economies and costs of living will not be easily comparable, so you'll have a more accurate insight into what you expect if you talk to other Brits in your field and see what the going rates are.

Commuting Culture

Particularly in London and larger cities in the UK, commuting to work by public transportation is hugely popular. Hardly anyone would drive into London for work (and if you do you'd fight traffic for hours and want to cry at the end of it), so people are much more used to being at the whim of delayed trains and tubes and buses.

It's very popular in a UK office to talk about your commute (mostly how bad it was because as I've mentioned, complaining together is a British pastime!).

This also means that, on the whole, people are a bit more receptive to lateness due to your commute if you run into a problem on your way in. They understand that you can't always plan for a broken down train or signal failure, and will probably commiserate with you rather than judge you as long as it's not an ongoing problem.

Christmas Pudding is Not Pudding
Celebrating Holidays in the UK

"Do you want some Christmas pudding?" Guy's mom asked on the afternoon of my first British Christmas. I, being my nervous expat self not wanting to turn down anything while equally being terrified at what I was getting myself into, simply responded, "Sure!"

I wondered what would make this particular pudding Christmas-y. Would it be dyed red? Green? Maybe come in the form of a present that you had to open before digging in to the chocolate or vanilla flavor?

When it was time to be served, I sat patiently, excited at this new cultural experience that was about to unfold.

Finally, a very dark and very cake-looking mound was set in the middle of the table.

"Here it is," someone said, "your first Christmas pudding!"

I looked around to see where it was, checking for any signs of a bowl of slightly jiggly, possibly vanilla or chocolate, pudding.

They were all fixated on the previously mentioned mound of…cake?

I was perplexed, but they all were certain that this was the Christmas pudding, so I imagined that the pudding must be on the inside.

Once I dug into my slice, I learned the cold, hard truth: "Christmas pudding," is not actually pudding, in the American sense. It's pudding in the British sense because pudding means "dessert" here, but this was not the wonderfully smooth chocolate pudding I had dreamed of.

This was…dried fruit and brandy compiled with some other exotic ingredients in a very dense cake.

I was momentarily shocked at the difference between what I expected and what I got, but everyone was watching me and so I had to dig in as if I wasn't phased.

"Mmm," I said as I choked down a raisin and my throat was lit on fire by the alcohol. "Interesting!"

I wept on the inside as I tried to figure out if all of my future Christmases would now be filled with this strange creation.

To me, the taste of Christmas pudding was that of sadness and liars. How could all of these people be excited about the prospect of eating this lump of regret?

This, by the way, is not a knock on the chef's cooking skills or ability to make a proper Christmas pudding. Judging by how great of a cook and baker she is, this was probably the best Christmas pudding that would ever cross my lips. If she were to take this to Great British Bake Off, I've no doubt she would win.

It's just that, as someone who perhaps hadn't grown up eating this particular dessert, I couldn't quite wrap my head around why anyone would willingly eat this combination of ingredients.

As it turns out, after extensive research among British friends and some high quality Googling, Christmas pudding is not necessarily loved for its incredible taste and texture. Many Brits I spoke to said that they only like their own mother's Christmas pudding, no one else's, and there are multiple articles online making fun of how "nobody actually likes Christmas pudding."

This confirmed my suspicions – British people weren't, as a whole, dying to eat Christmas pudding every day of the year. They liked it on that one day, after the Christmas dinner, because it was tradition. And sometimes, to a Brit, tradition just tastes good.

I'll get back to Christmas traditions in a bit, but for now let's talk about other holidays celebrated in the UK.

New Year's Eve

Besides entering the New Year five hours before the first parts of the US, Brits celebrate New Year's Eve in much the same way Americans do – fireworks, alcohol and staying up late to watch various celebrations.
Or, in my case, going to bed at about 9pm because I don't have the willpower to stay up that late.

The main focus of the national news coverage of New Year's Eve is focused on London and Big Ben, with revellers around the city singing "Aud Lang Syne" to ring in the New Year.

Each local area has its own traditions, however, ranging from "Hogmanay" in Scotland to the superstition in Yorkshire that you should say "black rabbits, black rabbits, black rabbits" as your last utterance of the old year and "white rabbits, white rabbits, white rabbits" as your first words in the new one.

If your New Year's Eve in the States used to revolve around coverage of the ball drop in New York City or televised parties across the US, you can always get some sleep and then ring in the New Year's again with your friends and family early in the morning UK time.

Valentine's Day

While celebrated in the sense that couples may get each other gifts or go out to dinner, Valentine's Day is not nearly as commercialized as in the US.

Children might bring Valentine's Day treats to school for their friends, but they don't necessarily celebrate it in the way many US students would have with bringing Valentines for the whole class and taking the time to make special Valentines mailboxes or other collection boxes to fit their treats in.

There will definitely be a push for chocolates, flowers, and lots of hotels offering a Valentine's weekend getaway deal if you are a fan of this "holiday of love."

St. Patrick's Day

While many Americans think of St. Patrick's Day as an Irish thing, it's actually more of an Irish-American "holiday." That's not to say that big cities in Ireland haven't embraced it and don't celebrate it, but it is by no means as extreme or filled with "stunts" like dying rivers green as sometimes happen in America.

The only UK country that would even remotely think about or celebrate St. Patrick's Day is Northern Ireland, and that is going to be mainly through parades and other festivities – not just pinching people if they're not wearing green.

In the other nations, St. Patrick's Day hardly makes a blip. Sure, if you're looking out for it or searching you may find some celebrations, parades, or pubs or hostels that have become "themed" for the night, but in terms of general acknowledgement of the holiday when you're out and about on the day, you won't find too much.

St. George's Day, St. Andrew's Day, and St. David's Day

Just like St. Patrick is the patron Saint of Ireland, England, Wales, and Scotland each have their own patron saint and day dedicated to them.

For England, this is St. George's Day which is usually on April 23rd unless April 23rd falls between Palm Sunday and the Sunday after Easter Day, in which case it's moved to be later due to a Church of England rule that no Saint's day can be held within this time.

For Wales, this is Saint David's Day, held on March 1st.

For Scotland, this is Saint Andrew's Day, celebrated on November 30th.

In each case, the day is usually celebrated by eating food and enjoying drinks from that country, perhaps flying the patron Saint's flag, and sometimes parades and dedicated programming on the television or radio. The only one of these celebrated as a national holiday (or bank holiday, as I'll explain below) is Saint Andrew's Day.

How, when, and where these celebrations occur near you will vary tremendously. Some years the day has gone by without me even noticing it happened, so this is not on par with Christmas or Easter when it comes to festivities, but definitely plan on searching out the celebrations to learn more about your new country and its traditions.

Easter

To understand Easter in the UK, you first have to understand that despite Christianity being the official religion in the UK, the UK is a much less religious country than America. So while your Easter memories and associations might involve dressing up and going to church (or at least seeing people around you doing that), you won't notice this same tradition in the UK.

That's not to say that people don't go to church on Easter – they do, but most people who go to church on Easter will be regular church goers.

Instead, on the actual day, families seem to jump straight into the egg hunts and family meal involving some sort of meat and vegetables.

The Easter Bunny is alive and well in the UK and is sure to visit the children and hide eggs, but the eggs he hides here are chocolate ones and not usually plastic ones with candy (or money) inside. Similarly, because the UK has brown eggs instead of white ones, the tradition of dying Easter Eggs is lost on Brits.

Easter ends up being a four day holiday in the UK, with both Good Friday and Easter Monday being bank holidays. This makes it a popular time to travel with time off work, whether to see family or to go somewhere abroad (my husband has fond memories of skiing during Easter time).

In fact, children in school actually get a lot more time for Easter break than just those four days – the "Easter holidays" are typically around two weeks in the UK where kids are off school. So Easter ends up being a significant holiday and time in a British person's life but not always for the same traditions and religious reasons as we would be used to in the US.

Bank Holidays

When I first moved to the UK and people talked about "bank holidays," I remember being confused by the term. It's one we don't use in the US, but it basically means the same thing as a "public holiday." That is to say that the various bank holidays throughout the year are officially recognized as public holidays and many workers get the day off.

There is not a requirement that your employer must give you the bank holiday off, but most sectors do.

Some bank holidays are holidays with a purpose behind them – Christmas Day and Good Friday, for example. Others are simply seemingly random days that are designed as a bank holiday (for example, one in May called the 'Early May Bank Holiday.')

England and Wales have eight bank holidays throughout the year, while Scotland has nine bank holidays and Northern Ireland has ten.

The best part is that if a bank holiday falls on a weekend, say Christmas Day on a Sunday, then the following Monday will also be taken as a public holiday.

Independence Day

Hopefully, it comes as no surprise that July 4th, or American Independence Day isn't celebrate outside of America. There is some celebrating to be found among American expats on July 4th, especially in London, but that is the extent.

Sometimes Americans have the impression that perhaps this will be a sad day or a day of resentment from the British, as if the Americas were the only colony that the Brits had ever owned and then lost.

Despite the fact that Guy finds it funny to try and convince Americans that Brits just skip July 4th on the calendar because it hurts too much, this could not be further from the truth. The British do not, in fact, care about July 4th, what it stands for, or the fact that America is no longer a British colony.

If I'm feeling particular patriotic on that day, I might bring something American into the office to share, and my coworkers are more pleased to dig into some cheesecake than worried about the past.

Halloween

Nowadays, Halloween has become much more engrained in British culture than in the past, but it is still nowhere near the level of excitement that happens over this holiday in America.

If you have kids, know that there is trick-or-treating in many areas, on October 31st, so they won't miss out on this tradition, but it isn't to the same scale and decorations are unlikely in most areas. As a kid, I remember being terrified to wander up to darkened houses where soccer dads were wearing monster masks and waiting behind bushes, ready to jump out at us while we were getting our candy.

For the most part, that kind of enthusiasm for Halloween just won't happen here. You may find some Halloween parties in major cities or where big groups of Americans live, but don't be surprised if you're the only one wearing your costume to work.

My husband has no memories of trick or treating as a child, which goes along with the narrative that Halloween really only began being "celebrated" in the UK in the past 10-15 years. This is supported by the fact that the annual "Fright Night" at Thorpe Park, a British theme park, didn't begin until 2002.

This isn't to say that you can't decorate your house for Halloween and get into the spirit of things, but just know not to expect the same from British friends or coworkers.

The cultural reasons for this are varied and worth reading up on if you have time, but the most practical one that seems to prevent Halloween from becoming bigger despite influences from across the pond is a British tradition that happens soon after Halloween on November 5th – Bonfire Night.

Bonfire Night

While Americans tend to have a reputation for liking to set fires and blow things up on various holidays (which is true), the British are not immune to this particular pleasure.

And since Bonfire Night in the USA isn't a thing, I thought it would be a good idea to explain the origins and celebrations behind Bonfire Night in the

UK as you will undoubtedly find yourself there during that time. After all, you don't want to end up like my friend who, upon hearing fireworks on Fireworks Night, promptly forgot it was a holiday and instead ducked and covered behind a bush.

History of Bonfire Night

Every year on the 5th of November (and the weekends surrounding it), the UK celebrates what is known as "Bonfire night," "Guy Fawkes night," or "Fireworks night."

The reason stems back to 1605 (typical Britain with traditions older than America itself).

Basically, the King at the time was Protestant, and the Catholics in England felt suppressed because it wasn't a time of "let's all love each other," but more of a "shut up, I'm the ruler and it's 1605 so I can do what I want" sentiment.

Anyway, Guy Fawkes was a part of a Catholic revolt group who had planned to blow up the House of Lords with gunpowder during the State Opening of Parliament on the 5th of November.

Fortunately for the King and the rest of Parliament, an anonymous letter went out that tipped off the authorities to the plan.

Late at night on the 4th of November, Guy Fakwes was found in the House of Lords guarding 36 barrels of gunpowder (not sure if the "it's not mine" excuse would have worked here) and promptly arrested.

Many of the co-conspirators of this "Gunpowder Plot" were hung, drawn, and quartered (hello, 1605), but Guy Fawkes managed to jump from the gallows and break his neck before they could execute him. How pleasant.

In celebration of the failure of the Gunpowder Plot and the fact that the House of Lords didn't go up in a plume of smoke and rubble, people started celebrating by way of bonfires and eventually it became a national holiday.

It was even celebrated in the North American colonies as 'Pope Day,' up until the American Revolution when we were like, "wait we're supposed to be celebrating religious freedom, not persecution. Let's find another day."

How the British Celebrate Bonfire Night

Nowadays, Bonfire Night has lost its religious tones and is just an excuse to get together with your town and light things on fire and eat hamburgers and drink.

Organized events take place all across the nation, and the bonfires are terrifyingly amazing.

People are invited to bring any wood or furniture that's being thrown out to add to the fire, and the firemen are invited to watch while the countryside burns as they drink mulled wine and help keep everything under control.

The end of the night is the fireworks display, where you hold hands with your loved ones, watch the children out of the corner of your eye to make sure they haven't gone face first into the bonfire, and do your best to time the ending so you're the first one out of the parking lot and don't have to wait in a long line of cars to get home to your warm bed.

Not quite the spectacle of the previous centuries, but British nonetheless.

Remembrance Day

Similar to Veteran's Day in America, Remembrance Day is a day each year that serves as a remembrance of the lives of soldiers lost at war. It began as Armistice Day, remembering the lives lost in World War I, but over the years has come to represent the lives of all British armed forces who lost their lives in battle.

This happens on November 11th each year, with planned minutes of silence across the UK and a ceremony in London attended by the Royal Family.

One of the big symbols of Remembrance Day is a red poppy. These red paper petals with the green plastic stem are worn as a symbol of support for the Armed Forces, and people begin wearing them in mid to late October up until and including Remembrance Day.

In recent years there has been controversy surrounding the poppies due to accusations that people wear them in a fake display of patriotism because everyone else is doing it as well. There are also groups of people who believe that wearing the red poppy is showing support for war (sometimes people will wear a white poppy to symbolize their support for pacifism and also remembrance of all who have died in war, not just the British).

As an expat, I do not choose to wear a poppy during the Remembrance Day period, though you are perfectly encouraged and allowed to wear one as a non-Brit.

Thanksgiving

One of the biggest letdowns for many American expats is living in a country that doesn't celebrate Thanksgiving. There is no reason for them to celebrate American Thanksgiving, of course, but I find that homesickness can really rear its ugly head when your friends and family back home are all together and you're stuck in your office trying to tell Olga why she needs to stop leaving her rotting food in the fridge over the weekend.

However, Brits are mostly aware that Thanksgiving exists in the US and may be up for having a bit of an event at work or in your social groups if you bring it up. When I was at QVC, they held a Thanksgiving lunch just for me and decorated my desk with photos of all-American things like Mary Lou Retton and cowboys.

I've also been to American Thanksgiving events held at churches and by local groups and there is a Thanksgiving service at St. Paul's Cathedral in London every year. American food stores will stock up on some of your favorites like pumpkin pie filling as well.

Thanksgiving in the UK is what you make of it, and the more you go searching for places to celebrate it and people willing to celebrate it with you, the more you'll find. I can't promise that you'll bring the Brits on board to enjoy your favorite creamed corn casserole recipe or finally understanding what macaroni and cheese is really supposed to taste like, but Thanksgiving can be a great time to introduce some Brits in your life to your traditions and infuse some of your home traditions to your new life in the UK.

If you're really worried about missing Thanksgiving or find yourself struggling every year, try to plan a trip back to the States for Thanksgiving so you can revel in the sights and sounds of the turkey and Macy's Thanksgiving Day Parade (oh, by the way, there are often places you can stream Macy's Thanksgiving Day Parade online so you can watch it sneakily in your cubicle or on your phone when your boss isn't looking – you're welcome).

Of course, with the lack of Thanksgiving comes a confusion surrounding

Black Friday. Traditionally, Black Friday has been an American occasion directly tied to having the days off for Thanksgiving, and for many years it was regarded as a strange practice by the Brits.

In recent years, though, UK retailers have tried to jump on the bandwagon with Black Friday deals. It is nowhere near the phenomenon that it is in the US, and those retailers that do have Black Friday sales tend to focus on the online market so people can shop from work as they don't have the day off, but you will see more mentions of "Black Friday" nowadays.

My favorite part of Black Friday, though, involves stampeding through a Target for $10 off of a $300 television with 8,000 of my other closest friends, and you just don't get that in the UK, so I've sworn off UK Black Friday altogether.

Christmas

If you celebrate Christmas, you'll be glad to know that it's the dominant winter holiday here in the UK. After all, with the official religion being Christianity, it goes without saying that Christmas pervades the culture, workplaces, schools and general festivities going on in December.

But if you're used to Christmas in America, then you might be in for a surprise when you realize that there are different traditions surrounding this very merry holiday (starting with the word "merry", in fact!)

Christmas Greetings

In the US, we're used to wishing each other a "Merry Christmas." Everything is "merry" and bright, and we use the word "Happy" when talking about things like birthdays, Thanksgiving, or a more general "Happy holidays."

The first time someone said, "Happy Christmas" to me in the UK, I laughed because it sounded silly to my American ear. They looked at me blankly and I quickly realized I needed to say something back and quickly recovered with a mumbled "Merry Christmas."

Over time, I've learned that "Happy Christmas" is the traditional Christmas greeting in England, which is thought to be because the phrase was preferred by the Royal Family and "Happy Christmas" became associated with being of a "higher class" – the class system in England strikes again!

It's not to say that Brits haven't heard "Merry Christmas" or that you won't hear it occasionally, it's just not the norm.

Christmas Decorations

Brits don't like to be seen as being too enthusiastic about anything, and when it comes to Christmas decorations, it's no different.

Yes, you will definitely see Christmas decorations up. And you are more than welcome to decorate your house however you like. But in terms of the great lengths Americans tend to go to try and make their Christmas light display the biggest and brightest in the neighbourhood, you won't find that here.

This is hard for me to adjust to because I love looking at Christmas lights around the holidays and if there isn't an inflatable RV with a half-deflated Santa Clause in someone's yard, I'm disappointed, but you can't win them all.

Father Christmas

Santa Claus doesn't do his rounds in the UK.

There, I said it.

But before you panic, you should know that he sends his alter ego, Father Christmas, to do his bidding. And he looks suspiciously like the American Santa Claus. Some more traditional versions have him with perhaps a bigger beard and wearing a blue robe, but in modern times he is a very close cousin to Santa Claus.

Except, as is the British way, he prefers brandy and mince pies (more on that in a bit) to milk and cookies. Leave it to British Santa Claus to be thinking about alcohol at such a pivotal time! Don't forget the carrots for the reindeer.

Presents

Similar to America, the "giving presents" day is typically Christmas day in the UK. Other countries in Europe, such as France, have their big celebration on Christmas Eve, but the UK more closely parallels the US in the "waking up on Christmas morning to open presents" tradition.

Pantos

While the American Christmas show tradition might be something like seeing the *Nutcracker* at your local theater, Brits have come up with their own Christmas play called the "panto." This is not one production – a panto is a family production that includes a lot of second rate actors somewhat following the story line to a popular fairy tale or legend like Peter Pan or Cinderella while singing songs and making jokes about the local area.

The very British aspect of a panto is that it's not supposed to be objectively good. The fun and the silliness comes in the audience participation, the "in jokes" that make fun of both the panto itself and the storyline, and the fact that there is definitely going to be a man dressed up as a woman at some point.

Sometimes, the sets are extremely elaborate and the effects are good – they are put on in very capable and larger theatres across the UK with experienced techs. They're just not supposed to be the best show you've ever seen – they're supposed to be a Christmas panto and nothing more, nothing less.

Drinking

The culture surrounding alcohol in the UK seeps into the Christmas season for many families. While this is individual to the person, of course, it's not unusual here to have friends get together and, well, drunk in the pub on Christmas Eve.

For many Americans, including myself, this was shocking. *It's Christmas Eve*, I thought. You're supposed to be home with your families or loved ones or your dog or whoever and be good and wait for Santa! Maybe have a Christmas Eve party with the neighbourhood while you get festive surrounded by decorations and food and drinks and Christmas movies.

You're not supposed to just go to the pub and get wasted!

But, as is the case with the Brits, particularly younger ones, that's exactly what they believe they are supposed to do and so Christmas Eve is no exception.

Christmas Food

As evidenced by my confusion at Christmas pudding, I had a lot to learn about Christmas food when I first moved to the UK.

The first thing to know is that the main meat for Christmas lunch/dinner here is usually turkey. With no Thanksgiving in the UK to stuff them with turkey in November, this has turned into their main festive meat on Christmas day.

Side dishes would likely be vegetables like carrots, Brussel sprouts, swede, and roast potatoes. You might also find stuffing, as well as a "Yorkshire pudding" which is essentially a baked flour batter that you pour gravy on or just enjoy by itself.

For dessert, the Christmas pudding will probably come out, along with crackers and cheeses. Again, this differs by family so if you find yourself enjoying a Christmas meal with a British family who brings out something different, don't hold it against me – I'm just telling you what can be classed as "traditional favorites."

One Christmas-time food that has mystified me for years is a "mince pie." Now, when I first say that, you may be picturing a large, meat pie.

Scratch that and picture individual tiny pies made most often without meat. Instead, the combination of dried fruit and spices is called "mincemeat" (trust me, I'm the one writing this and I'm confused too).

Mince pies are a very classic British holiday favorite, so they may be served on any day up into Christmas (people may bring them into the office to share, for instance), or they can be enjoyed as dessert on Christmas Day.

Christmas Crackers

One almost ubiquitous British Christmas tradition involves "Christmas crackers," and I don't mean like Ritz.

A Christmas cracker is a cardboard "popper" that has a small gift inside. When you pull the popper at both ends (typically by two people, on one each side), the cracker busts open and out falls your tiny, cheap gift plus a "Christmas hat."

The Christmas hat is a folded piece of a tissue-paper like paper that you can unfold and wear on your head like a crown.

Christmas crackers were invented in 1847 by a Londoner, so they have a long British history to speak of!

Village Fairs or Fêtes

Leading up to Christmas, Christmas markets are very popular in larger cities and "village fairs" are popular in the smaller towns and villages.

Whichever version you attend, you can expect stalls featuring local food, gifts, and possibly some games for the kids, as well as attendance by charities and other local businesses hoping to attract your business.

There are also often larger carnival games and maybe a merry-go-round for the kids.

Christmas Songs

The first time I tried to sing, "Grandma got run over by a reindeer" in my office filled with Brits, I was shocked by the lack of chiming in. As it turns out, British people don't like running Grandma over by a reindeer and aren't as familiar with that song as their American counterparts.

There are some Christmas songs that span both cultures – for instance, some of the more religious ones are sung in churches and what would the world be if we didn't all love Mariah's "Last Christmas?"

Others are country specific, like a song called "Fairytale of New York." Despite the American city in the title, I had never heard this song in the States and only got to know it when it played in the UK over and over again around the holiday season.

For a bit of a spoiler, the song includes an Irish immigrant sleeping off a hangover and a couple fighting about drug addiction, so – you know – apparently the typical Christmas in England!

Boxing Day

Celebrated on December 26th, Boxing Day is another bank holiday and important part of the Christmas season in the UK.

While in the States, we go back to our normal lives (and some of us are even back to work) the day after Christmas, Boxing Day is another day that Brits use to spend time with their friends and family.

There are often football (soccer) matches that take place on Boxing Day, as well as major sales in the stores similar to the US Black Friday (though still not to the same extent). If the weather is decent or at least tolerable (and the weather is often tolerable to a Brit who is used to the cold and darkness), people will go for walks in their local area or down to the pub.

It's also a great opportunity for families who saw one side on Christmas and are seeing the other side of the family on Boxing Day, either for a "Christmas Part 2" or to just get together. The food is often leftovers from the Christmas meal, or a similar meal with meat and vegetables (and of course leftover mince pies).

The origins of Boxing Day do, in fact, have to do with boxes – Christmas boxes. Traditionally, this was the day that the servants received time off to spend with their families, and the master of the house would give them a "Christmas box" which was a gift or perhaps leftover food from the meal to take home. It could also refer to Christmas boxes that were given to tradespeople like shoemakers and carpenters as a gesture of goodwill.

Today, typically no presents are given on Boxing Day unless you haven't seen that person yet to give them their Christmas gift, but the excuse to take a day off still remains!

I am definitely in favor of Boxing Day, as there's something depressing about ending Christmas Day in the States as life returns to normal. Boxing Day gives a nice buffer to transition from the Christmas spirit into the New Year and also, who doesn't love an extra day off?

What if I Celebrate Other Holidays?

The UK is so diverse, particularly in larger towns and cities, that if you observe other holidays like Hannukah, Ramadan and more, you will likely be able to find likeminded people or groups to get together with.

Just because the official religion is Christianity does not mean that this is at all mandatory or necessary.

Birthdays

If you're an expat for at least a year, there's one thing you can't get away from and that's having a birthday in the UK. Birthday celebrations here are not incredibly different than in the States, but they are often a bit less extravagant and unless it's an "important birthday year," may be celebrated with less fanfare than many people are used to in the US.

The one thing to know is that, on the whole, you are responsible for planning your own birthday, bringing in your own cake to work, and usually paying for yourself when you go out to eat for your birthday. In the US, it's more common to have the guests pitch in to pay for the birthday person's meal or for your co-workers to band together and get you a cake for your birthday.

It's not a requirement, obviously, that you do any of this – if you want your birthday to pass without anyone knowing or caring, you're more than welcome to do that. But don't just expect your birthday to be on everyone's calendars with surprise parties galore. As an expert party planner since I planned my own birthday parties from the age of about six, I'm fully on board with this birthday culture and encourage you to take advantage of it to make sure your day is exactly how you want it and who you want it with!

Squash is More than Just a Gourd
The Wonderful World of British Food

Have you ever cried in a produce aisle? I mean, really *cried*. And not because someone called you and alerted you to a death in the family or because some kid ran over your foot with the cart he shouldn't have been pushing.

Cried because you couldn't figure out what they called eggplant in the UK, or cried because you have no idea where to find the eggs or cried because they only stocked one brand of tortilla chips and what is that all about?!

The grocery store meltdown is a quintessential part of being an expat in the UK. It's like an initiation ritual that happens when you're all by yourself or with your unsuspecting partner, and there's no medal or certificate afterwards, just grocery store bleakness.

I mean, can we talk about how they don't even call them "grocery stores," but instead supermarkets? You're literally already behind and you haven't even stepped in the door yet.

My grocery store meltdown actually took a long time to come.

When I first moved to England, I was lulled into a false sense of admiration when it came to UK grocery stores. I marveled at the single sleeves of Oreos and the chocolate frogs and the fact that the eggs were never in the refrigerated section. Everything was new, and bright, and fresh, and I discovered that Sainsbury's chocolate chip cookies are the best thing that have ever happened to me and that potato waffles are in fact potatoes shaped into waffles, not waffle filled potatoes.

It wasn't until I transitioned from a student in the UK to a real person in the UK that the meltdown came. Suddenly, I had to actually buy real things at a grocery store like vegetables instead of tubs of Pringles.

One of the first times I went to the store, I had driven my car very delicately to the local Morrison's, proud of myself for being able to drive and getting myself to a grocery store in the middle of the suburbs without help from anyone.

Stepping out of the car, I felt the mist hit me in the face and the grey skies overhead were trying to crush my spirit, but I was being a real person in the UK and seemingly nothing could stop me.

That is, of course, until I got my cart and started in the produce section. This was a misstep for a couple of reasons, but namely because I still didn't have a handle on the differences in vegetable language. Zucchini is a "courgette" here, and eggplant is "aubergine," but I was too confident in my abilities and got courgette and aubergine mixed up when asking the friendly Morrison's man where to find the zucchini.

First of all, the fact that I couldn't find the zucchini was because I was like 22 and barely knew what a zucchini looked like, so I was looking for signs rather than for the vegetable itself. Be proud, mom.

"Excuse me," I asked very politely. "Where are the aubergines?"

He very helpfully pointed me to a section filled with eggplant. I thanked him, thinking that something had gone wrong in that communication transaction but I was already too British by this point to say anything or admit that I was confused.

I walked over to the eggplants, quickly realized my mistake, and then stood there, frozen in produce aisle fear. I couldn't remember the word for zucchini. And yes, I know you're reading this and shouting at me to just keep searching for something that looked like zucchini, but I was incredibly defeated and felt embarrassed that I couldn't even remember the name of a vegetable and it was all too much.

As I stood there, debating whether to continue the search, try and find someone who knew what a zucchini was, or abandon the mission altogether, I saw a bunch of watermelon.

And then I couldn't help but think of summers eating watermelon by the pool, soaking in the Florida sun and living the carefree childhood of a suburban American kid. I thought of my mom and how she would cut the watermelon, and how we would always buy the watermelon whole from Costco. I thought about the watermelon seed spitting contest we had in elementary school.

And that was it.

I cried in the produce section, and everybody helped me out in the only way British people know how in awkward situations: by ignoring me.

I tried to stop it, but the more I did, the more helpless I felt and the more those stupid watermelon were staring me in the face, reminding me of everything I had left behind.

And while the rest of this chapter is going to serve up some British versus American food truths to help you navigate supermarkets and grocery stores in the UK, I want to take the chance, again, to remind you that expat life is messy and weird. Emotions are all around you, even in the produce aisle, and you know what, if some watermelon set you off, so be it.

Foods with Different Names

One of the main hurdles you'll jump over as an expat is figuring out the different names given to foods in the UK versus America.

In order to make this as easy as possible for you to refer to, I've compiled some of the most popular ones in list form. Copy it down to take to the store with you and you'll be all set!

US   -   UK
Zucchini…courgette
Eggplant…aubergine
Rutabaga…swede

Cookies…biscuits
Mashed potatoes…mash
French fries…chips
Cotton candy…candy floss
Cilantro…coriander
Cupcake…fairy cake
Oatmeal…porridge
Chips…crisps
Candy…sweets

Brands You Won't Find in the UK

Despite my best efforts, there have been many American food brands and types of food that just aren't available in the UK unless you shop in the American import section and want to pay like five pounds for a box of cereal, which, no thank you.

I do not claim to have gone to every single store searching for these products, but, in general, you should expect to find different brands in the UK.

Some notable absences include many sugary cereals – the UK cereal section is much smaller than in the US, which parents who don't want to rile up their kids with a sugary start will appreciate.

You also won't find Pillsbury products, Ore Ida potato products, Koolaid, fruit gushers, or white cheddar popcorn (hello, Smartfood, call me, I've got a proposal for you). Microwave popcorn is nowhere near as prevalent, and peanut butter is definitely available but with fewer options than you would expect in an American store.

There are also no Goldfish, no Cheez-its, not such a huge emphasis on pretzels, and finding a dill pickle can be a real challenge.

Where Can I Find American Food in the UK?

If you're desperate, and you will be at some point, you should know that there are some American food stores you can order from online in the UK (just do a Google search), and if you're near a large Sainsbury's, Tesco's,

ASDA, or other grocery store, you should be able to find an "International foods" section which often have some samplings of American food!

Is it expensive? Of course it is. Is it worth it? When you're like ten seconds away from an expat meltdown that could be solved by a Chocolate Chip Cookie Dough Poptart, absolutely.

Why Are Eggs not Refrigerated?

When you try and find the eggs in a British grocery store, you'll notice two things that make them different from their American counterparts – and no, it has nothing to do with the chickens having a British accent.

Firstly, the eggs aren't in the refrigerated section. They're just sitting in the regular aisles, many times near the bread. To an American, this is horrifying as we grow up with eggs being a food item that you most definitely refrigerate. In the UK, though, the process that the egg goes through means that it doesn't need to be refrigerated to prevent salmonella. This compares to the US where refrigeration is an important part of making sure your eggs are safe to eat, so don't get all crazy when you visit the US and try to keep your eggs room temperature.

The other difference you'll easily spot is that the eggs are usually brown, not white. While this makes egg dying at Easter difficult, you might be surprised to know that white eggs were prevalent in the UK in the 50s and 60s. The transition to using hens that lay brown eggs was a consumer-driven one.

Consumers equated white eggs to less healthy or factory-produced, similar to how you might view white bread as less healthy than brown bread. Stores caught on, and over time realized that the British public really wanted brown eggs, so that's what they got!

Sometimes, the differences in America and Britain comes down to small cultural shifts that turn into bigger movements with no complex reasoning behind it. Brits just prefer brown eggs, even they don't taste any different!

Typical British Food

Much like how each state in America has its own traditional food, and even more specifically, each city has the culinary creations its "famous" for, Britain is no different. The traditional breakfast in England is slightly different than the one in Scotland, and the types of food enjoyed by locals differs on the region.

Part of the beauty of being an expat and really feeling like you're getting to know the UK is to explore these things on your own, but I've pulled together some information on some of the most traditional foods so you can get prepared.

Squash

Less a traditional food and more something you'll find in almost every British person's home is squash. And I don't mean the yellow gourd that Americans associate with Thanksgiving and cartoons of pilgrims bringing it to the table.

I mean the fruit-flavored concentrated syrup that you add to your water to give it a different taste. Squash comes in a plastic bottle and includes flavors like orange, blackcurrant, lemon and many more.

It's not meant to be enjoyed by itself – the syrup is so concentrated that you just need a couple of splashes in a drink.

I mention this because the first time someone offered me "squash," I pictured being saddled with a giant yellow gourd to eat all by myself rather than having one glass of flavored water. I emphatically told them "No, thank you" while they looked confused as to why I seemed to have such an aversion to squash.

Now that you now, you can go through your British life not making the same mistakes I did and perhaps even find a new drink you enjoy!

Creams

Brits love cream. It's just a fact. They eat it with dessert, often, probably because British cake is typically much drier than American cake and you need a bit of liquid to be able to get it down.

In the UK, heavy cream is called "double cream" and half and half is called "single cream."

Sunday Roast

A "Sunday roast" is a traditional meal often enjoyed on, surprise surprise, a Sunday! Brits like to equate it to an "American Thanksgiving meal every Sunday," but I don't buy that comparison. What it is is a form of meat, either chicken, beef, pork or lamb usually, combined with vegetables like carrots and roasted potatoes, sometimes stuffing, gravy, and sometimes a Yorkshire pudding like the one we talked about in the holiday section.

These types of meals are often enjoyed in the winter months, but can be an all-year round occasion. It's a real "event" that you can invite other people to as well – for instance, "Hey, do you and your husband want to come over for Sunday lunch?"

Fish and Chips

If you don't know that fish and chips are associated with Britain, then you've been living under a rock and I need you to come out now. Possibly the most British meal of all, fish and chips is enjoyed all over the country no matter how far from the coast you are.

The main fish used is cod, but you can also get haddock or plaice in some…places.

And chips, of course, are chunky fries (and I mean, chunky!) They're not usually very crispy, but slightly mushy. Oh, and speaking of mushy – the trifecta is completed with some mushy peas!

The fish and chips takeout place (called takeaway in the UK) is known as a "chippie," and you'll almost always get better fish and chips there than in a restaurant that serves other things.

Traditional Breakfast

In England, you often hear of a "traditional English breakfast" and the same goes for each of the other UK nations – there are small variations on exactly what type of food is included in a traditional Welsh/Scottish/Irish/English breakfast, but overall you can expect some type of toast, eggs (usually fried), mushrooms, beans, and tomatoes. Sausage or bacon are also staples, and then each country will have their individual additions like the potato scone in Scotland, seaweed puree in Wales, and potato bread in Northern Ireland.

People don't usually start every day with traditional breakfasts if they work a non-physical type of job, but it is a treat for people at weekends and when they want to really indulge themselves.

Black pudding

One of the least understood but most often talked about UK foods among visitors is black pudding. To keep it simple, black pudding is a combination of pork, dried pig's blood, and fat.

I will leave it up to you and try!

Scotch egg

As evidenced by the name, Scotch eggs are a delicacy in Scotland but also in the rest of the UK. The basics are that it's a hard-boiled egg covered in sausage and meat and breadcrumbs and fried or baked. You can make them yourself or just buy them in supermarkets.

Pie

When a British person asks you if you'd like some "pie" for lunch or dinner, they're not offering you a sweet pie like apple pie or pumpkin pie.

Instead, they're talking about a "meat pie." Popular types are chicken and leek pie and steak and ale pie, but there can be many meat and vegetable combinations.

It makes sense, as the UK can be a cold place and meat pies are good pub food to help warm you up!

Chip butty

For the first couple of months I lived in the UK, I would hear Brits make fun of American food and how bad it is for you – they were amused at my Pop-Tarts for breakfast, affinity for sugary cereal and the "deep fried everything" they had seen on documentaries about the Midwest.

I went along with this for a while, until learning that UK food can be equally as deliciously unhealthy, and who in the world were they to talk when they had invented the "chip butty."

This is, for all intents and purposes, a french fry sandwich.

Literally two pieces of bread or a roll, buttered, plus fries in the middle and condiments.

A sandwich.of.french.fries.

After learning of this culinary delicacy, I was in UK food heaven and feel grateful for their contributions to my carb intake.

Egg and soldiers

I've included egg and soldiers because I had no idea what it was when my husband first introduced it to me, but I also think it's a great way to give a mini-lesson on the cooking of eggs in the UK. There are different methods and words than we usually use in America.

So, to start off, "egg and soldiers" or "dippy eggs" is when you have toast cut up into slices (the soldiers), and dip these into the runny yolk of a boiled egg.

It's a popular kid's dish in the UK, but I like it too, so sue me.

Brits in general will often have their eggs fried, usually with the yolk still runny, known as "over easy" in America. If you want the egg fried but the yolk also cooked through, you would need to explicitly state that as there isn't really a term for that here.

Other egg terms, like scrambled, boiled, and poached are all applicable in the UK.

Other British Food Oddities: Explained

Here's a lightening round of British food fast facts you should know!

British pancakes are more like crepes – less fluffy.

Scones are sort of like biscuits, but more dense. The version of an American biscuit that you think of when you think of a fluffy biscuit doesn't exist in the UK.

Sandwiches in the UK include popular ingredients like prawns, chicken, cucumber and cheese (not in those combinations!). You'll have a hard time finding a turkey sandwich in the UK!

Bacon in the UK is thick bacon, a bit like a tough ham, rather than crispy bacon that you'll find in the US. US style bacon is called "streaky bacon," and you still need to request for it to be almost burned to resemble US bacon.

What's the Deal with Afternoon Tea?

Somewhere along the way, Americans got it in their heads that Brits just stop for afternoon tea each day to enjoy a spread of fancy things like scones and crumpets and cakes from a floral teapot.

This is wholly untrue, sadly. While tea is a big part of British culture, you're not really going to enjoy a full afternoon tea unless you purposefully go to book one for a special occasion.

You should try one, of course – I've had countless afternoon teas since moving to the UK just because it's something to do with friends and family and who doesn't love a finger sandwich?

Just don't expect it brought to you on a platter at work or your mother-in-law's house or anything.

Baking and Cooking in Britain

If you like to hang out in the kitchen and whip up some culinary or confectionary creations, you should keep in mind that your oven will be measured in Celsius, and many things in the UK are measured in grams.

My husband gets absolutely furious when he's trying to make an American recipe – "a cup of flour?" he'll yell. "WHAT IS A CUP? A BIG CUP? A SMALL CUP?"

You should also do a quick search for different terminology before heading off to the grocery store. For instance, cornstarch is called cornflour, powdered sugar is called icing sugar, and all-purpose flour is called plain flour.

British Restaurant and Pub Culture

British Eating Culture

Especially outside of London, there is a slower pace to British life than in the US, and that doesn't stop when it comes to the culture surrounding eating.

For many months after I first started eating dinner with my husband's family, I would get so antsy after we had finished dessert as the conversation would continue for sometimes up to two hours afterwards. Sometimes, the conversation lulled and I looked around incredulously to try to understand why everyone was still sitting there, and then someone else would say something and it would continue again.

My husband got annoyed at me plenty of times because, in his words, "I looked like I wanted to be anywhere else."

I found it hard to articulate why I was so out of my element until he experienced a dinner with my best friend and her boyfriend at the Cheesecake Factory (which is sadly not in the UK, bless my broken little Cheesecake Factory loving heart).

At the end of the meal and after finishing off our ridiculously sized cheesecakes, we paid the bill and my best friend and I gave each other the look of " it's time!" and got our purses and stood up to go.

I looked over at Guy, who was snuggling himself into the corner, prepping himself for the "after meal" part of the meal.

He was startled a bit by us all getting up, but quickly followed suit. As we walked out to the car, he said, "I get it now."

"Get what?" I asked, trying not to throw up from the thousands of calories I had just stuffed in my mouth.

"Why you're always so antsy after a meal," he said. "Americans end it so abruptly!"

Again, as I will say a thousand and one times in this book, it's impossible to make a generalization about all British families or how all British people eat. But after speaking with other expats and observing many different Brits enjoying meals together, I feel confident in including this as something to be aware of.

A meal, to a Brit, is not just about eating, but about socializing and spending time together. "But that's what I do to when I eat with my family," you might say. And maybe you do. But as a whole, the end of the meal comes a lot faster for Americans than for Brits, and this took my introverted and impatient self some getting used to.

Another difference is the timing of meals. Brits don't do as some European countries do and eat at 9pm or 10pm at night, typically, but they do eat both lunch and dinner a bit later than Americans.

Breakfast would be the same in both countries pretty much whenever you get up and need to have it, though you could expect to enjoy breakfast in a café from about 7am to 10am (McDonald's goes until 10:30am here if that's anything to go by!)

Then, lunch is typically taken around 1pm, with dinner happening around 7 or 7:30pm.

I was used to eating dinner in the US around 5:30pm or 6:00pm (and sometimes even earlier), so this was an adjustment for me, but I'm proud to say that I haven't starved yet.

Eating in Restaurants

The concept of what a restaurant is is pretty much the same in the UK as in the US, though it could be argued that the US has more "well-loved" family chain restaurants than in the UK. My husband finds chain restaurants in the US infuriating, because he just wants to try the local food, while I try to explain that the local food of Winter Springs, Florida is bagel bites from the local Costco so he should sit down and enjoy his Olive Garden before I tell the waitress he doesn't want any more breadsticks.

In the actual restaurants, though, you go in, get seated, and are given a menu just like in the States. Some places let you book ahead, others don't, but you'll figure out quickly which ones of your favorite local restaurants book up early.

After your meal is done, you'll find that you aren't instantly brought the check (or the bill as it's called in the UK).

This goes along with the "after meal" being an important part of the meal here. You are typically not going to be rushed out and they will account for the fact that you will sit there after your meal into their booking schedule. To a Brit, bringing you the bill before you ask for it is a sign of rushing you and is not good service.

This is, of course, another area you can make a cultural blunder, as often to an American, not bringing the check after the end of the meal is a sign of bad service!

When you do ask for the bill, know that you can choose to tip or not.

There isn't the same "tipping culture" in the UK as in the US and everyone in the restaurant should be earning minimum wage if not more, so it is not a social requirement to tip, and you only do so if you feel you've had great service.

Even when you feel on cloud nine about the service you received, tips hover more around 10 percent than the American 20 percent and up.

Pub Culture

Pubs are a huge part of British social life – unlike a bar, most are open to families, at least up until a certain time, and it's not uncommon to have a work lunch at a pub either. They are truly a center of what keeps life moving in the UK and so it is of course necessary that there is somehow food involved!

Pubs serve both food and drinks, though they will often have specific hours for ordering food, so don't expect to show up to any country pub at say, 4pm, and expect there to be food on offer.

Another thing to know about the pub is that you need to go up to the bar and order, rather than a waiter or waitress coming to you to take your order. The number of times I see groups of American study abroad students waiting anxiously in a pub for someone to come to their table and take their orders is indicative of how not-used to pub culture we are as Americans!

This also means that you don't need to leave a tip at a pub, as no one is coming around checking on your table or taking your order in a traditional pub.

Separated by a Common Language

Deciphering British Communication Styles

It was 2011, and while I hadn't dreamed up my plans to live in the UK yet, the language confusions were already beginning.

I worked at a summer camp in Pennsylvania alongside other 20 something year olds from around the world. There was a large contingent of international staff, including British students who used the summer camp work as a way to travel the US.

One afternoon, as I was in the office, a camp counselor came in looking desperate.

"I need a plaster," he said, holding his hand that was dripping with blood.

We looked at him, confused

"Why do you need plaster?" someone asked, wondering if he was going to make a cast of his hand for a wacky camp project.

"I've cut myself," he said, gesturing to the obvious wound now getting bigger. "I need a plaster! Do you know where I can get one?"

"I mean, they might have plaster in the art building, but you need a Band-Aid first," someone else said.

As she fished out the Band-Aids from the First Aid kit and handed them over, it soon became obvious that we were talking about the same thing.

"Oh, he said. What did you call that? A Band-Aid? We call it a plaster. Thanks!"

Back then, he was the one out of his element, trying to communicate to us in a language we didn't understand despite it also being English.

When I eventually made it to the UK the next year, it was me in the hot seat, wondering at every turn if I was going to make sense to the people I was speaking to.

Language differences are a huge topic for new arrivals to the UK, as it's one of the easiest ways of explaining that no matter how much the UK and America may seem alike on the surface, there are often differences you may not even be aware of until you actually experience them.

This crops up over and over again, no matter where you live or work. Some language differences are easy to understand based on context and America's access to British movies, celebrities and television shows.

Who hasn't heard Gordon Ramsay call something "rubbish" or one of the *Harry Potter* characters use the term "Bloody hell!"

The bigger confusion comes in when you start hearing words that aren't necessarily words you would hear throughout the day. For instance, if someone asks you for a brolley, would you know they were searching for an umbrella or would you think they're looking for a weird kind of trolley like I first did when I heard that word? If someone told you to put your finished paper in their pigeonhole, would you know that they meant their work mailbox or would you think they raised pigeons?

It would be impossible to present you with an exhaustive list of language differences that I've encountered over the years, and it would be doing you a disservice anyway as part of the fun of being an expat is having those embarrassing moments and figuring things out for yourself.

But I will share one of my language snafus so you can both laugh at me and protect yourself from that particularly awkward moment, and then I've provided a list of some of the more important language differences to know.

Pants and pants

I have never been a fashionable person, but I have caught on over the years that the best way to make new friends is to compliment something about them even if you have no clue if their outfit actually looks good or not.

Keeping this in mind, I was in a class at UCL, a university in London, where I knew no one and was trying hard to make at least one friend. A girl sat down next to me wearing bright purple jeans, and something in me knew this was going to be my opportunity for striking up a conversation

She pulled out a pen from her stylish backpack and arranged her note taking set up as the professor was at the front trying to figure out how PowerPoint worked. I knew that this was my chance – get in with her before the lecture starts and then we could spend the whole time making side comments to each other and laughing to ourselves when the technology goes wrong and the whole auditorium has to troubleshoot the PowerPoint.

I leaned over, ready to put my plans into action. "Hey, I like your pants!" I said with a smile, gesturing towards her jeans. I waited for her to return the compliment or at least smile. Instead, she looked down in her lap and then up at me.

"Thank you?" she said, almost as if she was asking why I had said such an offensive thing. I was taken aback by her inability to receive a compliment and resigned myself to the idea that perhaps I didn't understand the social rules of speaking to people in lectures. Or maybe British girls just didn't know how to take a compliment.

When I told my study abroad advisor this story the next day, she revealed the key piece of information it would have been great to know before I made a fool out of myself.

In the UK, pants means underwear.

Oh.

Some British Words to Know

US...UK

Around the House

Stove...Hob
Backyard...Garden
Closet...Wardrobe
Attic...Loft

Clothing and Accessories

Underwear...Pants
Pants...Trousers
Tennis shoes...trainers
Flats...pumps
Umbrella...brolley
Stroller...pram

Transportation

Truck...lorry
Trunk (of a car)...Boot
Gas station...petrol station
Highway...motor way
Provisional License...Learner's Permit

Informal Greetings

Are you alright?

Another area where American expats can make themselves look like fools (in the best way possible) is not understanding certain British greetings and phrases. From "cheap as chips" to describe something that's inexpensive to "just popping out" when they say they're going to leave for a short time, the Brits have their own idioms that you'll learn along the way. Some are easier to understand than others from context, and others, like "Bob's your Uncle!" will leave you scratching your head (it means 'you're all set', for the record).

But of all the British phrases, there is one that stumps Americans time and time again – not because we're wildly misunderstanding it, but because we think we know what it means when we don't.

That phrase is, "Are you alright?" or shortened to "Alright?"

To an American, we would ask this question of someone when we are concerned for their well-being. Maybe they've been distant lately, maybe they fell over, or maybe we know they're going through a hard time. Whatever it is, when someone asks you "Are you alright?" your heart grows a few sizes when you realize that that person truly cares about you.

On the other hand, when a Brit says "are you alright?" it means something similar to "What's up?" – a greeting with no emotion behind it besides acknowledging someone's existence. This is simply a "hi," a "how are you" that does not actually want you to go into any detail about how you are. Unlike the American way of using this phrase, it's not really a question.

I was so impressed when I first moved to the UK that everyone cared so much about me, but as it turns out, they didn't really at all! Or at least, they weren't showing it by asking me if I was alright.

To respond to "You alright?" you can either just say "yes, thanks!" or "yes" or "good, thanks" or respond in turn with "yeah, you alright?" I choose some of the former as I think I sound a bit silly saying the latter with my American accent, but you might be a braver expat than me.

Oh and on the topic of British greetings, "Cheers" both means "thanks" and is something you can do at weddings when you "cheers to the bride and groom." To respond to the "cheers" as a thank you, a simple "no problem," "sure!" or "you're welcome" will do just fine.

The "x's"

Part of language in the 21st century involves the written word, and I'm not talking Chaucher, I'm talking texting.

I'm including this bit because it absolutely confounds Americans who move to the UK and I still have to double check with my British friends about how to communicate this way, so buckle up.

In America, many people might sign off with an "xo" or "xoxo." This could be in a text, e-mail, birthday card, whatever. But you're most likely only going to use it as a real show of support or sign-off. Most people don't send messages like, "we need milk xoxo" or "what time are you coming over? Xoxoxo"

Brits, on the other hand, have incorporated their form of sign-offs, the "x" meaning "kisses" into text messages in a very confusing way for us Americans.

See, there is a hierarchy of "x"s, with one "x" meaning "we are just platonic friends and maybe barely know each other" to like five "x"s which you would probably save for a best friend or significant other.

The problem comes in when people can't seem to agree on how many "x"s mean's what! I get "x" as a sign off from families that I work with in a professional capacity, and then I feel like a horrible person for responding without an "x" as if I'm slighting them somehow!

For some real trauma, consider a situation where you're "talking to" a Brit in the early stages of dating. Not only do you have to try and play it cool in so many other ways, but you've also got to spend hours googling "how many x's" mean "I like you" to make sure that you're not giving off weird vibes.

And to overthink it even further, as an American I'm almost always worried that Brits will know that I don't use "x's" in regular texts to other people so they'll think that I'm just trying to copy them or pretend that I'm British when I'm really not.

To solve the problem, I've started using the smile emoji as my sign off, which I think says, "Hey! I'm American and don't know how many 'x's to use, but I want to show you that I am writing this text message or e-mail from a place of kindness and I still like you, don't worry."

Indirect Communication and Saying Sorry

In addition to the different words they use, Brits tend to operate in a communication culture with a lot more subtext than in the US. They don't always say what they mean or mean what they say, and the art of passive aggression and sarcasm is alive and well across the pond.

For you, this means that there may be times when your boss may say something like, "can you e-mail Matt when you get a chance?" and that means to e-mail them straight away. Or maybe someone who has their arm cut off comes up to you and says they've got a "bit of a problem."

Get used to digging a bit deeper into what they say to make sure you get the full picture.

The stereotype about Brits saying "sorry" all of the time is also true. The old example is that if you were the one stepping on a British person's foot, they'd be the one saying sorry. Saying "sorry" in the UK doesn't always mean that you're actually sorry. It can be a placeholder for something like "hey, move your bag please!" or "Can I get past you?"

Ultimately, it's about showing an outward display of politeness, even if you're seething inside.

The Dish Fights
Figuring Out Cross-Cultural Relationships

A dishwasher saved my relationship.

I don't say this because of the practical benefits of a dishwasher, though of course there are many.

I say this because the number one source of real, day-to-day tension in my cross-cultural relationship has to do with this one household chore.

It's not because neither of us want to do it (which we don't), but because our thoughts on the mechanics of how to do it probably explains why America had to find independence from the UK in the first place.

My husband was taught to wash dishes by filling the "washing up bowl" with water and soap, turning off the water, and then washing all of the dishes in this bowl. He'll swap out the water occasionally, but not until it really looks like a swamp of leftover food pieces and spit. Rinsing happens, but doesn't seem to be a necessity.

This method of cleaning up isn't unique to him or a knock on him. He would argue that it saves water, thus helping the planet, and that there is not a dire need to rinse the dishes because they've already been washed and the soap will just dry off.

When I'm on dish duty, I may or may not fill up the sink (not the washing up bowl because I think they're stupid) with water first, but I'm definitely leaving the tap on the other side to help wash and rinse as I go. I'm of the opinion that this helps prevent washing dishes in a bowl of dirty water, and I do not want soap film as a side when I'm enjoying my dinner.

As it turns out, these two methods of cleaning up reflect our cultural upbringings, as I've found time and time again that Brits take his side and Americans, mine.

It would be okay if we could laugh it off and let the other get on with their dishwashing lives, but we're incapable of watching the other wash dishes without going into a rage – him at all the water I'm wasting, and me at the piles of murky water my plates are being submerged into.

If I could compile the number of fights we've had and separate them by topic, the dishes would be the clear winner.

Ultimately, no matter how hard we tried, our preferences for this task were something so engrained in us that there was no amount of "seeing the other person's point of view." We could meet in the middle on so many things, but when it came to the dishes, we were prepared to go to war to fight for our corner.

When we finally moved into a home where we could have a dishwasher installed, it was our first purchase.

The magic of having an appliance that would wash the dishes without us needing to feud over it helped us begin to migrate our arguments to new things, like the correct occasion to use a paper towel.

Whether you're currently in a cross-cultural relationship and have your own version of the dish fights or you're still waiting on your dream British significant other, this chapter will help you navigate the wonderful world of dating, falling in love with, and marrying someone from across the pond.

Dating

When it comes to dating in the UK as an expat, you might feel a bit out of your depth not understanding some of the cultural cues or practices. I mean, a first date is hard enough, but a first date when you can't understand why you were brought cake when you ordered "pudding" is worse.

Overall, as with any culture, people are people and as I quickly learned, there was not one common trait that "British boys" had. The dating process, like anywhere, involves getting to know the person for who they are and not acting according to the stereotypes or past experiences you might have with people "like them."

However, there are a few generalizations that I will share, not to put British people or the British dating scene in boxes, but to give you some overall insight.

Appearance

From the workplace to classrooms to the dating scene, Brits tend to be more fashion forward and dressed up than Americans. At the end of the day, you shouldn't be dressing up in clothes you feel very uncomfortable in to go on a date or go out somewhere, but you should definitely make your best effort and check the dress code of the venue ahead of time so you don't show up to a fancy afternoon tea in flip flops.

Ways to Meet People

Especially in the larger cities, it can be difficult to date and meet people naturally after you spend your time commuting and working or studying. One of the often repeated options is to join clubs and meet-up groups surrounding your interests, which is a good idea when it comes to even making platonic friends.

Another method of meeting people that has really taken off in the UK is online dating and using apps to connect with people who you want to go on a date with. It's not seem as shameful or embarrassing, and many people use it as a way to connect with others in a purposeful way. It also appeals to British reserved sensibilities as it means you don't have to be socializing with 100 different people at all hours of the day to meet the love of your life!

PDA

Unlike some European countries, public displays of affection are not generally appreciated in the UK. No one is going to do anything more than give you a few annoyed looks if you do find yourself making out on Oxford Street or something, but it's seen as better manners to keep your affection private.

Of course, people still hold hands and kiss each other goodbye and you're not going to need to walk on the other side of the street to your date, but be aware of how your British partner feels about PDA before engaging in any as they might find it too much.

Communication and Banter

Brits are known for their "banter," which is basically a quick wit and back-and-forth conversation filled with teasing by way of insults. I have always found this slightly jarring to my American sensibilities, and it took me awhile to really understand how they communicated and when they were just teasing (all of the time) and when they actually felt that way (none of the time – usually if a British person doesn't like something about you they're usually not going to say it to your face).

When it comes to dating, do your best to keep up, but if you find yourself getting lost in the conversation or not understanding what they're meaning, just make a joke out of it and play the "confused American" card.

Cross Cultural Relationships Advice

Whether your attempts at dating Brits has gotten you a relationship while you're an expat or you find yourself moving to the UK for a British partner, I think we'd all agree that cross cultural relationships come with a lot of emotional and practical landmines. It's a flurry of "oh my god, I just love your accent" and "oh my god, can you please just rinse the soap off of the dishes, you monster."

Here's what I've learned about cross-cultural relationships since being in a fairly functioning one where we only want to kill each other over cultural misunderstandings like twice a week.

Appreciating Different Histories

Every person's life and relationships are shaped by how they've grown up and what they've done in their lives prior to knowing you, but you tend to have a lot more in common when you were both raised in the same country. Even if one of you grew up in Texas and one in Massachusetts, your shared history as Americans with a lot of the same cultural cues will give you some automatic starting ground.

When you're with someone from another country altogether, their history and past life seem very foreign to you because it literally is.

There are the "practical understanding" things, like when Guy tells me about his school days and uses terms like "A Levels" and "Headmaster" and "GSCEs" and I have to try to keep up or the references to past movie stars or singers that were popular in the UK that didn't quite make it over to the US.

Then, of course, there is a sort of unspoken way of viewing the world that is very different when you have people from two different countries in a relationship. For instance, I, like all Americans, have a real emotional reaction to September 11th and found it incredibly insulting when Guy would put forward some theories he had heard about the event and even so much as suggest that there was so much as a mistaken word in the news about what happened.

To me, this was a part of my history as an American and one that I didn't want someone else speculating about. To him, it was a world event that happened in another country that he felt, like many other world events, he was allowed and entitled to research theories about. He didn't lack a cultural understanding of the event – it was just that his was from the perspective of a third party country witnessing the day rather than being terrified in your fourth grade classroom when you heard that someone was attacking your country.

Appreciating the past history of the other person and how their views have been shaped goes a long way towards understanding each other.

"Your" Way is Not Always Right (except when it comes to the dishes)

As I mentioned in the introduction, Guy and I's number one fight relating to our cultural upbringing has to do with washing the dishes. Once we had a dishwasher come in and play the peacekeeper on that particular source of disagreements, we moved on to the next topic: which cloth to use in the kitchen.

Now, every household is different so it's not a cut and dry "British versus American thing," but overall, it's safe to safe that Americans use a lot more paper towels in the kitchen than Brits (who call them 'kitchen towel').

I have been conditioned, both by my upbringing and by endless commercials, to use paper towels to clean up many spills in the kitchen. Sauce all over the countertop? Paper towel. Water on the floor? Paper towel. If I'm in a real bind and can't find the dish towel to dry a dish? Hello, Bounty!

Guy, on the other hand, has been taught (like many Brits) to use reusable cloths in the kitchen to clean up. He would use the cloth, rinse it out a bit, then leave it hanging in the sink until it dries and can be used again tomorrow. These get washed as they get "too dirty," but "too dirty" is a very wide definition!

To me, I appreciate the "save the environment" aspect, but also feel like a reusable cloth spreads dirt around and doesn't soak up liquids as well as a paper towel, while his perspective is that using paper towels is a waste and reusable cloths are much sturdier.

If you can imagine, then, that if we're together in the kitchen cleaning up, there are some judgmental looks and "why are you using that?!" Sure, we could just let it go and let the other person use what they want to, but that wouldn't be as much fun and also we're much too invested in our own ways to not comment.

This is a classic example of one of those times where our upbringings and cultural environments have created two different people who do things differently and just can't see eye to eye on the best way to do it.

Other differences include driving (he doesn't see why I prefer an automatic when a manual transmission wastes less gas) and tipping (he can't comprehend the fact that people pay extra on top of paying for the service, and I can't rid myself of American tipping culture where I just want to give them all my money).

Over the years, we've navigated this by trying to compromise where we can and accepting that the other person does it differently when there is no logical compromise to be made.

As much as I don't agree with some of the way he does things around the house, I also know that it doesn't feel great when he's telling me that I'm doing it wrong either. You don't realize how things are ingrained in you until you are living with a person who does it completely differently, but the best advice I could possibly give is to pick your battles. It's not all worth fighting over, and sometimes, just sometimes, it could be that your way is the one with more downsides!

Don't Use Their Nationality as a Weapon

Guy and I joke around with each other about our cultural differences. It's impossible for him not to be amused at how crazy we Americans are about some things, just like it's impossible for me to not laugh at some of the very British things I observe.

The problem comes when you're using each other's nationality as an insult in a moment of anger or homesickness. Talking about how "Americans are crazy" when he's telling me why he doesn't want to move to America isn't helpful, and me going on about how "British people are so depressing" when I'm feeling homesick is equally not great.

When you communicate in moments of anger or frustration, try to pinpoint the actual behaviour or situation that bothers you rather than resorting to a clash of Americans and Brits.

Explore Both "Homes"

While this book covers moving to the UK from America, the same holds true whichever country you're living in: introducing each other to your home countries and hometowns is an important part of making a cross-cultural relationship work. I found that before Guy had been to America and my hometown, it didn't feel like he was a part of my life in the same way I was his. He hadn't met my friends, my parents, my family or seen any of the places that were important to me, and without that connection, I couldn't bring that part of myself to the relationship in the same way he could.

Showing an interest and making the effort to explore your British partner's world is an important way of showing them that you're committed to learning more about them as a whole and complete person, but don't forget that it goes both ways.

In a healthy cross cultural relationship, your partner or spouse will also want to see and get to know the part of America that is important to you and make an effort to meet and befriend the people that you hold close in the States.

After Guy's initial visit to America, he has come with me once or twice a year. Sometimes I prefer to go on my own just to catch up with my friends and family for a short visit, but he does visit regularly on his own accord and not just because I beg him to.

On our last visit, we took a trip to Texas to see one of my best friends for a couple of days and spend a blissful weekend talking to her and her boyfriend and doing very Texas things like drinking sweet tea and feeling like we were seconds from dying every time we drove on the highway.

On the return trip home, he said to me, "I feel sad that you don't get to live by your friends. We should have them come visit and they can stay at our house whenever they want."

It might not seem like a lot, but it meant the world to me. Being the person who lives away from their home country can be extremely difficult, but knowing that your partner is supportive of this other part of your life can be the difference between the relationship flourishing or not.

Being the "Trailing Spouse"

When you do find yourself in the situation of having moved over to the UK for a partner, whether that means for your British partner or for your American partner's job, it is very easy to feel out of control of your life very quickly.

Despite the fact that I stayed in the UK on my own free will, a part of why I did was because of Guy, who was my boyfriend at the time when I was figuring out what my future was going to look like.

Sometimes, we make decisions for people that we love that don't always put our best interests at the forefront, for instance if your partner gets an amazing job in the UK while you have to leave your awesome career behind. In those cases, we prioritize our relationship over ourselves, and that can be a beautiful and wonderful thing.

It can also make you absolutely crazy and resentful and jealous of everything they have and you seemingly don't, so there's a fine line to walk.

At this point in my expat journey, I do have many days where I want to move back to the US, and if I'm being completely honest with myself and with you, there have been months and years where these days tend to outnumber the ones where I want to stay in the UK.

Guy, on the other hand, made it clear from the very beginning that he wanted to live in England. I agreed to this, at the time, because England was new to me and exciting and I thought I wanted to live here forever.

For us, navigating this situation has been complex and fraught with emotion, but we have come up with some ideas about working remotely that will help us move forward and figure things out once I get my permanent UK citizenship and don't have to worry about visas anymore.

For others, this is a very difficult issue that involves kids, careers that can't be done remotely, and many other considerations.

To be the one who wants to move to America while your partner doesn't can be devastating – you realize that you are not on the same page about a big life thing and that can be terrifying.

The only possible way to navigate this situation is to be honest about your feelings before they build up to an absolute loathing of the other person. You cannot be in two places at once and a family doesn't work quite as well when it's separated by an Atlantic Ocean, so it might feel like there's no "right" solution, but getting it out in the open without being whiney will make a world of difference to how you feel and how you're able to talk about it and deal with it.

Sometimes, relationships just aren't strong enough to withstand the pull of one partner to go back "home," and while I think it's a really sad thing, I do think that you shouldn't spend your whole life being unhappy and you have to do what works for you to find that happiness. There is a giant, massive, blinding caveat, though, that I've also discovered that many times the feelings of unhappiness are attached to you, not the place, and so moving back to America may seem like it's going to solve everything, when in fact you're just dealing with the same feelings in a different environment.

And while you're trying to navigate your life and figure out where your heart is really happy, make sure that you show your British partner (or your American partner who loves the UK) that you are making an effort to make friends, get a job or just enjoy yourself in the UK, even if it's not your ultimate happy place.

I've found that my concerns and thoughts about living in America are taken even more seriously by Guy when I'm not in the throes of homesickness and I have shown that I am trying to feel my way through expat life. A bit of understanding on both sides goes a long way.

Lectures Aren't Mandatory (But You Should Go)
Navigating UK Student Life

I started out my journey in the UK as a study abroad student, which is really common among American expats. Whether they came abroad and met the perfect person and fell in love or they ended up getting a job in the UK, being a student is one of the best low-risk ways to get introduced to life here.

There are multiple types of students in both the undergraduate and graduate sphere, with the undergraduate study abroad students coming abroad for the shortest time typically. This was how I first started coming to the UK, for four month stints at a time. If that's you, this first section is for you. If you're coming on a graduate degree or are direct enrolling at a UK university for your entire undergraduate degree, skip to the next section.

Undergraduate Study Abroad Students in the UK

Choosing a Program

If your university gives you choice in your study abroad options and you haven't chosen yet, picking a program can be extremely daunting. Not only did you have to narrow down your destination city, but now you have to pick a program based on factors you're unsure of, seeing as how you've never been to the UK and can't exactly travel there to assess every program before you get there. So how do you make more of an educated choice and less of a shot in the dark?

If you have the option, I would always advise choosing (or start out with, in my case), your university's sponsored program. For instance, the University of Pittsburgh offers a "Pitt in London" program, one of its most popular programs. Not only do credits usually transfer more easily, but your university has done this dozens of times before with previous students who have your background and understand what it takes for its students to thrive in the UK. It also gives them the opportunity to do orientations and allow you to meet people you'll be living with beforehand.

But what if your university doesn't have a specific program and the option is up to you? Most universities will limit it to just a few UK options to make sure you go with a legitimate provider that will give you the necessary documents to transfer credits back home. So, okay, you have two to three options, but how do you choose between them? If your university has allowed you to choose them, the basics are already covered in terms of safety and legitimacy. I would still do your research, of course, but unless your university is sending you to "Bob's London College N Things," you'll probably be set.

Cost

If you're on a budget like I always was, cost may be the biggest factor, in which case your "pick a program" exercise is pretty simple. Not all programs are alike in cost (one year I was deciding between a $14,000 program and a $19,000 program, which was one of the easiest decisions of my life). Also check the 'add-ons.' Is it possible to buy your own flight and save money? Are there additional costs outside of what they've put down that you'll be responsible for? One of my programs included a full London travelcard for the whole program, which is a huge cost that was worth having included.

Type of School

If cost isn't a factor, investigate where you'll be studying. Study abroad program "providers" can either have their own location (such as CAPA London), or they will act as your mentors while you are enrolled at another university (API London, for example). Will you be studying at a British University or at an American university with only other Americans (and this matters, but we'll talk about that in a second). Is it near the major sights or is it an hour tube ride away? Does the school have a good reputation? You have to decide what your top factors are here because it's going to be different for everyone. If you have options in your study abroad program, then it's similar to the process you went through to find an American university. What fits you might not fit someone else—just pick somewhere you feel you'll thrive.

British University vs. American University

This is one of the biggest differences in study abroad programs, and an important one to pay attention to. There are plenty of American universities in the UK, and many are specifically set up for study abroad students. My first study abroad experience was with CAPA, who had their own study center, professors, and classrooms for students. However, they weren't a "university" and you couldn't sign up to attend CAPA as a "regular" student. I also studied at Richmond, the American International University in London. This is a "regular" university that takes both American and British students. However, they also play host to plenty of study abroad students through a study abroad program provider.

Then you have "direct enrol" programs or exchange programs where you are enrolled at a British university just like any other British student. Some of these programs will provide you with some sort of American 'assistants' who live in your city and organize events and will help if you need it. When you're truly direct enrolled, of course, (for example if you decide to do a postgraduate program and apply independently as an international student), you may have an international advisor, but you won't have any specific "American" support.

Why It Matters

The reason these distinctions are so important is because it can make or break your study abroad experience. Living and studying with only Americans is a much different atmosphere than living with studying with British students and other international students, and while there is no 'right' choice (notice a theme?), it's something to consider.

Many students prefer to study with a large group of American students (at either an American or British university). There's something about being in it "together" that makes a short term study abroad an incredible bonding experience. One of my best friends was one of my roommates during my first term abroad, and many people have the same story. You have people around you who understand any culture shock you're experiencing, and it's comforting to know that you're not alone.

On the other hand, does anyone really move to the UK to spend all of their time with Americans? You could do that so much cheaper in America! The benefit of a direct exchange or living with British students or international students is that you get the "real" experience, not an insular version of what life in the UK is like. This option pushes you out of your comfort zone and encourages you to make friends with people who have completely different backgrounds to you, which is what study abroad is all about.

As I've said, neither way is correct, and you really have to know your personality to know what you'll prefer. My first program was with a large amount of American students, and my second program was a "direct exchange" where I was the only study abroad student on my floor. In hindsight, the reason I did a direct exchange for my second program was because I had gained a confidence in myself on the first. I would not have thrived as a direct enroll student my first time in London, as I would have felt lonely and had a difficult time making friends. But some people are just the opposite; living with Americans in a foreign country would be far too 'safe' for them, and they would thrive in a direct exchange environment. Know yourself, and don't be afraid to choose the environment that you'll feel most comfortable in while still giving you room to explore your new home culture and grow as a person.

Graduate and Undergraduate Direct Enroll Students

After working hard on my first essay for my Master's degree in the UK, I stared at the results with my jaw dropped. A 72 percent? How could I have received a 72 percent after I had spent multiple weeks tweaking this essay to be the best essay that had ever essayed?

I wanted to cry and crawl under my covers so that I wouldn't have to face what was surely my failure in the UK, and I began figuring out how I would tell my parents that I was dropping out of my Master's degree.

I texted my British friend who had gone to the same university I was studying at (oh yeah, Brits call all higher-education "university"). "I got my first essay back," I said. "I can't believe it."

"What'd you get?" he texted back.

"A 72," I said, with about 26 sad emojis to really emphasize my plight.

"Good work!" he said.

I was taken aback. Why was he being such a sarcastic jerk in this very sad moment?

"Don't be mean!" I said. "I'm really upset about it!"

"…" he texted back. "How could you be upset about that?"

At this point, I thought something might be slightly up.

"That's a bad grade," I said.

"It's an amazing grade," he said.

I wasn't quite sure who to believe in the moment, so I embarked on some quick internet research that I really should have done before starting my degree.

"Oh," I texted him back once I started reading. "A 72 in America would be terrible!"

Before we get too deep into hashing out the differences in grading systems and what led me to almost have a mental breakdown over what was apparently a good great, let's get some of our higher educational terms straight.

Terminology

Going to school in the UK is a real trial by fire and new terminology and phrases. The education system isn't just different in the UK, but it's also talked about differently.

For example, you would never say "going to school" to mean college in the UK, as "school" is what they would think of as lower levels of school like elementary school and perhaps the middle school age. Another example is that the American "semester" or "trimester" is called a "term" in the UK.

You also wouldn't say "college" to refer to college in the UK, as they call it "going to university." A "college" in the UK is actually the name for where some students would go after they finish their required schooling at age of 16 (more on that later).

Within university (which is usually three years as opposed to four years in the US), you would choose an area of study, but it's not called a "major." So let's say you were going to study English, you would say "I'm doing English at university" or "I'm studying English" rather than "I'm majoring in English."

When you get those grades back on said English degree, they're also usually called "marks" or "results" rather than "grades."

Other differences would be that a "course" in the UK typically refers to the entire degree you're doing rather than just one class, and the word "class" isn't often used – it's either a "lecture" if you're being talked at and a "seminar" if it involves discussion.

The words for the staff at the university are different as well, with a "lecturer" being someone who gives the lecture and a "tutor" being a member of academic staff who gives you academic guidance and support throughout your degree. They won't tutor you in the American sense, but will instead give you feedback on assignments and help you adjust to university academic expectations.

Grades/Marks

Despite me feeling like a 72% was a failing grade, it was actually on the top end of what was possible in my UK degrees. The UK also uses 0 to 100% to grade papers and exams and projects, but at university they do not refer to grades as "A," "B," or "C" like we do in the States.

Instead, UK universities refer to grades as things like "First class," "Second class" or "Third class" and have other breakdowns like "2:1" and "2:2" (with a "2.2" being a worse grade than "2.1")

When you do get a percentage, you might try to immediately equate it with your normal US grade, in which case you should know that around 70% to 100% is the equivalent of an A in most US universities, with it being almost impossible in many degrees to get higher than around a 75% or 80%. A 50% to around a 70% is equivalent to a B (with the higher percentages representing something an A- or B+ and the lower ones representing a B-).

The passing mark is about a 40%, and beneath that, typically would be equivalent to an "F."

The best thing you can do is make sure you're aware of your UK university's grading system from the very first day you step foot inside.

It's easy to see, once taking a look at this grading system, that the UK university life is not at all similar to the US university life when it comes to grades, and the differences just keep coming from there!

Teaching Style

When I was at the University of Pittsburgh, which is fairly representative of a standard college or university in the US – meaning it wasn't a very small liberal arts college with its own grading system or unique educational approach – I was used to being given assignments, readings to complete, possibly quizzes along the way, and then an exam at the end. The exam could be in the form of an essay or short answer or multiple choice (thank God the geology class I took was multiple choice because to this day I still know nothing about geology).

Other projects could include group assignments, short research projects or regular papers throughout the class. I also got graded sometimes on participation and could earn "extra credit" in a few instances. While I could choose my essay topics sometimes, for the most part I was told what to learn and when to learn it so that I could pass my classes and succeed.

The first time I stepped foot into a UK college level class, I was given what was referred to as a "reading list" and looked at it with horror – there must have been 20 book titles on there, and I was only there for one semester. After a brief panic, it was explained to me that this was a list of recommended books that would help guide my studies, not an exact prescription on what I had to read. It was expected that I was interested in the subject and so would use the reading list as a base off which to do my own research.

Doing my "own research" was something that really stood out as the main difference between UK and US universities. In the US, I had more class time than in the UK, but was expected to do less outside of class than in the UK. In the UK, there was a focus on self-directed learning – there were not going to be multiple pop quizzes and participation grades as I went along. Most of my grade would come from either a single exam or perhaps one paper and one exam. There were no second chances, no person telling me I had to read up to page 50 by class next week, and oftentimes no direction on what I should write my essay about.

This can be a hard transition if you are used to an American education, but once you get the hang of it, it can be incredibly worthwhile and a freeing way to experience learning.

Dissertations

In America, we think of a dissertation as something done by a PHD student, but in the UK, they are completed by both undergraduate and graduate students at the end of their degree. This is not applicable to every degree, but it is for the majority of them and you can tell when it's the end of the year on social media in the UK because there will be lots of photos of students turning in their dissertations physically to the university's office!

The idea behind most dissertations is that you complete original research on a topic of your choice related to your subject. You will work with your tutor to establish what your topic is and then it's up to you to do polls, surveys, interviews, experiments and other research methods to come up with your conclusion and argument.

Student Life

Student life in the UK and US are similar in some ways – everyone on campus is pretty much broke, for starters, but the college experience on a UK campus is very different to that on a US campus, and understanding these differences will help ensure that you're making the right choice for you, or at least are prepared for them.

Length of Degree

The biggest difference about the UK and US student experience is that in the US, you get one more year of it!

UK undergraduate degrees most often last three years, as you specialize in your subject from Day 1 rather than taking additional classes unrelated to your subject. Most American undergraduate degrees, as you well know, last four years.

The same goes for Master's degrees, with most UK ones lasting one year and most US ones lasting two years.

Student Loans

The cost of a degree is much less expensive in the UK – for one year at a top university, you're looking at about just under £10,000 if you're a UK resident. For international students, this goes up to £18,000 to about £30,000 per year. Comparing this to the University of Pittsburgh, which is neither the cheapest or most expensive of US colleges, this is either cheaper or similar pricing. And when you think you only have to pay for three years in the UK versus four years in America, well, suddenly it makes sense why some Americans dream of doing their degree in the UK!

If you're an American student directly enrolled at a UK institution, you often will be able to get US loans to cover your costs, but I also wanted to point out the difference in the use of the phrase "student loans" because you'll hear Brits mention theirs and it can be slightly different.

In the UK, there are student tuition loans which would pay for your tuition, but there are also maintenance loans which give you a set amount to go towards cost of living. This is what most Brits refer to when they make jokes like, "Student loan came in today! Going to Primark!" I was taken aback when I first heard everybody talk about spending their student loan on dinner and not their tuition fees, so now you know!

It's also helpful to know that American students are not eligible for those loans that a Brit would get.

Drinking Culture

Because the age of legal drinking in the UK is 18, there are a lot more school sanctioned drinking activities that take place at a UK university, starting with "Freshers" week where the "first years," as they're called in the UK, come to campus early to take part in orientation sessions and basically parties.

This can be a real adjustment for an American who is used to 21 being the legal drinking age, and was a bit jarring for me when I realized that British students liked to go out a lot more than I experienced on my American campus.

Extracurriculars and Sports

American universities thrive on "extracurricular activities" and sometimes, as in the case of sporting teams, these are actually the true pride and joy of a university legacy rather than the academic stats. From Friday nights spent watching the football team against your rivals to the omnipresence of fraternities and sororities, the "university experience" takes place outside of the classroom, in many cases.

This is not the case in the UK, where college sports and mascots are all but non-existent, and while you can get involved in sporting teams and clubs and societies, these are looked at as a small portion of your university life in many cases. Sororities and fraternities do not exist, and the expectation is that you spend your time either studying, in class, or socializing and out with friends (not in an organized setting).

Now, don't get me wrong – there are places to get involved on UK university campuses – from musical theater to volunteering to science societies, you can find places to do "extra" things and there are student unions where you can hang out and possibly attend meetings, but you won't find the same level of extracurricular involvement as you do in the US.

Living and Eating

Everyone's got to live and eat in college, but the way you do is a little bit different in the UK and US.

In the US, most people share a room with their college roommates when they live in dorms, and this is an expected and normal part of college life. In the UK, dorms are called "halls," you usually only live in them your first year, and you have your own room in the vast majority of cases – Brits raise an eye when I tell them that in the US I once shared a room with two other girls in it!

British universities also usually have less emphasis on dining halls than in the US – again, there is a wide variety of set ups so this is not strictly true everywhere, but oftentimes there will be no "food plan" involved and the dorms are "self-catering" with small kitchens to share. And even when there is a dining hall, you will hardly ever encounter an American style dining hall with options for like 18 different countries and a buffet of food just waiting for you to dig in.

Wedding Breakfasts are Not Breakfasts
Understanding What the Heck Goes on at a UK Wedding

I'm just going to throw it out there. I did not expect to marry a Brit when I first came over here.

I mean, yes, I had seen all of the *Harry Potter* movies and thought that British accents were basically the classiest thing in the entire world.

But I didn't expect to marry a Brit. I met my husband, Guy, through a mutual friend while I was a student on my second study abroad program. We had both worked at the same summer camp in America, Camp Lindenmere, and our friend Rebecca knew us both as she was a camper when Guy worked there and a counselor when I did.

On the night of our fateful meeting, my mom and my friend Rebecca were in town at the time and I had conflicting plans. On one hand, Rebecca invited me to go with her to meet up with her "friend from camp," while my mom also hoped to spend some time with me. I debated about what to do, but eventually ended up going to dinner with Rebecca and her friend.

Luckily it worked out, as that night started the relationship that turned into an engagement that turned into a marriage and a life abroad.

When we began to plan our wedding in 2017, however, it became quickly apparent that Americans and Brits had very different expectations when it came to this romantic day.

See, I was used to a "do what you want" kind of wedding. If you wanted to get married on a beach, barefoot, well congratulations, you can do that. If you want to get married on a mountain with goats surrounding you while standing on your head, you're probably not the first one. Americans take a much more open approach to weddings and what they "should" be.

Brits, on the other hand, have a very specific wedding formula that goes something like this:

In the early afternoon, everyone shows up to the church or registered wedding venue if you're having a civil ceremony (you can't just get married anywhere. It has to have a roof and be registered. Because. Just because).

Then you do the ceremony, which, if you're having a Church of England wedding, is about 45 minutes and includes a lot of pre-planned wording that you can't deviate from or you won't actually be married at the end of it.

If you're having a civil ceremony, it's a bit less strict.

Then, ceremony over, throw some confetti at you as you leave the church or venue, and everyone off to the reception (called the wedding breakfast – I'll explain in a minute).

There's often a cocktail hour before the reception where you feed people miniscule amounts of food and lots of alcohol, and then you go into the sit-down meal. After the sit-down meal featuring some sort of chicken and profiteroles, speeches are done (often just from the men, though this is changing) and then eventually as the night wears on it turns into a dance party and everyone gets drunk and doesn't remember what happened the next day.

The night typically ends at about midnight or a bit later, and the scheduled end time is listed on the invitation as "carriages at XYZ time." Sadly, these are not real carriages, but simply a phrase.

Now, I have to make clear that if this is the way you want your wedding to be, more power to you. But there's no real denying that this is the format of a standard English wedding.

When we started our wedding planning, it became very apparent very quickly that a typical English wedding was my absolute worst nightmare. I don't like dancing, I don't like drinking, I don't like feeling too formal, and I don't like going to bed past about 9pm.

Luckily, Guy had an open mind and we were able to come to a compromise about what our wedding format would be. We ditched the stuffy format and held it in a horse's retirement home (seriously). It started before lunch, at 10:30am, which is basically unheard of over here.

The amount of comments we got about our start time, you would have thought that we told everyone we were getting married with paper bags over our head.

"10:30am?!" they would proclaim in shock. "But my hairdressers don't open until 10:00!"

Um, okay? Sorry?!

Eventually we got people to come around to the unusual time, but this wasn't the last time we came up against some judgement on the way we wanted the day to go. I was completely shocked the whole way through at how attached an entire nation seemed to be to the way a wedding was "supposed" to be.

I was surprised again when it came time to plan the ceremony.

"I can't wait to say 'I do'" I said.

"I don't think we say 'I do' in England," Guy said.

Cue my shocked face.

It's true. In a Church of England wedding, you say "I will," not "I do." And that iconic line that's in every American movie, "You may now kiss the bride?"

NOPE.

Just as I was coming to grips with this new script, I also learned that the bridesmaids and groomsmen (referred to as 'ushers') usually sit down at the front of the room instead of standing up next to you as you're getting married.

That was too much for me, and I put my foot down. There was no way I was getting married with my bridesmaids sitting down next to me rather than standing up, and while this all sounds very bridezilla now, it was a very real struggle at the time to assert what I felt was my "Americanness" into the wedding. I didn't want to give up on some of the very essential and core parts of the day I had always envisioned just because I was getting married in a different country.

Thankfully, we were allowed to have our bridesmaids and groomsmen stand during the vow exchange, and while we had to squeeze them awkwardly up there, we got it done.

The English/American divide showed its head again when we were talking about wedding cakes.

It's tradition in England to have a fruit cake on your wedding day, which is not surprising given the general penchant for cake with fruit in it in England.

When I heard this, I was horrified.

Fruit cake?! We don't even eat fruit cake. I hate fruit cake! Why would we have fruit cake at our wedding?

Spoiler alert: we ended up having two cakes at our wedding - fruit cake and chocolate cake, made lovingly by my now-mother-in-law.

Not because we liked fruit cake, but because it was tradition. This is just what you do.

That attitude cropped up quite a lot during our wedding planning, and it really helps to explain a lot of how I learned to relate to my life here. Some things are done because that's the way they've always been done. Weddings are early afternoon, not in the morning. You have fruit cake at your reception.

I do want to say, for the sake of family members and friends who may be reading this book, that every family member and friend who took part in our day was unfailingly accommodating and willing to bend the rules a bit (a lot) for me. They may have started thinking that weddings are fruit cake and all night drinking and dancing, but they at least looked like they were enjoying themselves at our very not-English morning wedding and I will forever be grateful for that. It probably didn't hurt that we had free drinks.

If you're planning one or attending one anytime soon, here are some of the major differences between American and British weddings, explained!

Hen Party/Stag-Do

Brits refer to the bachelorette party as the "hen party" and the bachelor party as a "stag-do." As far as I can tell, there are no hens at a hen party and no stags at a stag-do, just a bunch of drunk people.

In both countries, these parties can be one night events at a local bar, or they can be longer vacations or weekend getaways. Or they can be whatever you want - I had a day with my bridesmaids where we went out for an afternoon tea, saw a play, and then had dinner.

We also may have stopped at the Disney store because I have no shame.

"Where's your hat?"

One of the most visual differences between British and American weddings is that it's traditional in Britain for women to wear a hat to a wedding.

Many of the younger women I saw wore smaller 'pinned' hats that looked more like giant barrettes (they're called fascinators), but some did wear full floppy hats.

It's a classy tradition, but can make the view of the ceremony slightly obstructed with colorful feathers. There are worse things in life.

There is no such tradition in America, and hats are not particularly common things to wear to a wedding.

Wedding breakfast

The reception dinner in England is referred to as the "wedding breakfast," not to be confused with an actual breakfast. There is nothing remotely breakfast-like about the wedding breakfast, trust me.

The first time I attended a British wedding, I was very excited for some eggs and hashbrowns and was subsequently very let down.

The reason it's called a wedding breakfast is because breakfast is the first meal of the day and this meal is the first meal that the bride and groom will be enjoying as husband and wife.

As you can probably guess if you're British, Americans call it the "reception dinner," because, well, it's a dinner that takes place at your reception. Got to keep it simple!

Bridesmaids and Groomsmen

In the UK, a groomsmen is referred to as an "usher" and is in charge of helping guests to their seats and performing similar duties.

The wedding party in the UK also tends to be smaller (two or three close friends as opposed to the 3+ you would expect as the norm in America).

There is still a best man and maid of honor in both countries, and brides and grooms will typically choose the person closest to them whether that's a friend or family member to stand in that role.

A-List/B-List Invitations

One of the most shocking differences between American weddings and UK weddings boils down to who gets invited.

At a typical American wedding, you have one invite list who are welcome to join you for the entire day.

In the UK, you would usually invite closer friends and family to the actual ceremony and invite less-close friends or acquaintances to the reception only.

I have to say, as both a "full day" and "reception only" guest recently, I much prefer the American style of "you're in or you're out."

It feels a bit awkward to know where you "ranked" in the bride and groom's life. This is a wedding, not the Hunger Games.

Bride Comes in First

In America, it's always portrayed that the bride walks in last after her bridesmaids. This is the "grand reveal," the big moment, the "why we came" sort of event.

In the UK, the actual traditional way is for the bridesmaids to walk in after the bride, holding her train.

This isn't necessarily always the case nowadays and has been mixed from the weddings we've been to, but it is a difference to be aware of.

Wedding Start and Finish Times

Weddings in America typically start...well, whenever you want! But often they start in the late afternoon or evening and go until around 11pm or so.

Weddings in England usually start around lunchtime or just before, and they go...ALL DAY AND NIGHT LONG! Literally, from, say, 1pm in the afternoon to 1am in the evening.

When I first moved to the UK, I was shocked by this. I've always known weddings to be about a five or six hour affair, not an entire day! But Brits love to party, so the wedding just...doesn't stop.

The Whole Family Doesn't Walk Down the Aisle

Okay, so another difference between American and British weddings is that while the *whole* family doesn't usually walk down the aisle in America, you often have a procession of the family, including the mothers of the bride at the start of a wedding to get everyone into their places.

Perhaps the groom and his mother will walk in hand in hand or something similar.

In the UK, this is most definitely not a thing. The groom hangs around the venue before everything starts and then gets into "position" once it's time to roll.

The only people who typically walk down the aisle are the bridesmaids and the bride with her father or whoever else she wants to have walk her down the aisle.

Wedding Venues

Did you know that one of the main differences between UK and US wedding is where you can actually do it?

In America, you can get married wherever you want. It's not the venue that makes it a legal event, it's the officiant (more on that later).

My mom got remarried while in a backyard, my friends have gotten married while on the beach, and I always dreamed of getting married in the middle of a field somewhere under a tree.

In most of the UK, you cannot legally get married anywhere without a roof. So that means that outdoor ceremonies are not actually official, unless you have a gazebo with a roof over it.

Even wedding venues that are inside have to have a wedding license before you can legally get married inside them.

Who's the Officiant?

In the UK, the rules surrounding who can marry you vary depending on if you're having a religious or a civil wedding.

If you're having a religious wedding, than the church vicar would likely be the one to officially marry you, and if you're having a civil ceremony, there will be a licensed registrar who marries you on the day.

In America, there are many more options when it comes to who can be the one standing up in front of you marrying you.

Almost anyone can take a course and be licensed to be an officiant, and we've been at weddings where everyone from friends to family members to old teachers or coaches marry the couple.

Gift Registries

Registries really depend on the part of the country you live in and what is normal for that area, but typically Brits live together as a couple before Americans would.

Many American couples, especially in the South, still live separately until they get married, so their official wedding registry would be filled with things for their first new home together.

In a country where living together before marriage is much more popular and expected (I mean, the cost of rent in London is enough to explain why), many people choose to have cash registries or honeymoon registries where you contribute to a person's honeymoon or other fund instead of buying them household items they already have.

Open Bar

Depending on the region you live in in the US, it can be considered very tacky not to have an open bar at your wedding. The thought of asking people to pay for their own drinks is considered rude in many places, and you factor in this cost when it comes to planning.

In the UK, whether because people drink so much that it would be unaffordable to offer this or because the wedding usually goes on longer, it's often the norm to have guests pay for their alcoholic drinks at the bar. You would often serve alcohol with dinner and then again for toasts, but when you're late into the night and people are dancing away, the cost is on them

Sort Codes will Sort You Out
A Bunch of Useful Things to Know

Not all of the things expats encounter fit into nicely laid out categories. To celebrate the fact that expat life isn't always organized (or something like that), here's a collection of a bunch of "other stuff" that you should be aware of!

What Not to Bring to the UK

If you haven't made the move yet, listen up. Spare yourself and do not bring hair dryers or hair straighteners unless they are enabled for "dual voltage" (and most aren't). You run the risk of blowing up your products and nobody wants to be left with singed hair or a fire caused by your own vanity.

You also should be very selective about your furniture. Remember what I said about UK houses being smaller than American ones? You don't want to bring over too much and find that you only have a tiny strip of floor space to walk on. Check the dimensions ahead of time and be mindful of what you're better putting into storage than schlepping over.

UK Customer Service

Working in customer service in the UK was a strange transition for me coming from a consumer culture that usually says the "customer is always right." Americans are used to a high level of customer service wherever they go, and if a business lacks that, it can be a quick farewell to them because they just won't last.

From employees following you around in Target asking if you need any help to waiters and waitresses stopping by your table often, it's easy to get used to being "looked out for" as a consumer at every turn.

In the UK, you won't usually encounter this same level of customer service. My end-of-month reviews as a customer service employee in the UK centered around how many refunds I had given to customers – the fewer, the better. While I would have gotten a speaking to if my customer satisfaction scores were incredibly low, the real aim of the game was to keep the customer decently satisfied while not giving away too much of the company's money (even though the problem was never caused by me to begin with).

You also won't find employees hounding you in stores asking you if you need help, and sometimes it can feel like your waiter or waitress is never going to come back and ask if you need anything.

This is the nature of life here and what Brits see as acceptable customer service – my husband is always shocked in America by how far he has seen companies go to keep my service.

Certain places here, like John Lewis (a department store) can make names for themselves based on the high level of customer service they promise. When not everyone is doing it, it's easy to stand out for it.

As an American expat in the UK, it can sometimes feel like companies don't care about you or value your business, but if you lower your expectations just a bit, you'll figure it out just fine. Take it from me and the time I embarrassed myself by asking for a new sandwich at an outdoor restaurant because a wasp landed on mine.

I have since become much less precious.

Buying a House in the UK

Once you've lived in the UK for awhile, it might be on your horizon to attempt to buy a house. The Brits are obsessed with home ownership to a much larger degree than Americans, and if you're establishing a long term life here, the security net of owning rather than renting is tempting.

As an expat in the UK, there are ways that you can buy property, though your chances are higher the longer you have lived here and it depends how long you have remaining on your visa. With little exceptions, banks want to see either "indefinite leave to remain" or to see that you're on the track towards settlement. Someone on a shorter visa that does not lead to settlement is not a great candidate for a mortgage because in the eyes of the bank (and the Home Office), you should be returning to the US shortly.

If you are on the road to settlement and want to purchase a house, you should know that the way house purchasing works in the UK is different than in the US. For starters, "real estate agent" isn't a term – it's just the "estate agent," and there are not "seller's agents" and "buyer's agents." There are only agents, and these agents work for the seller.

The exact process is slightly different in each country, but in general, if you're listing your house, you will go to an "estate agency" and have them come around and value your house. They will list it on the market for you, and they will take care of the viewings. Once they have found a buyer for your home, you will use a solicitor (lawyer) who is trained in the house buying process. They will work with the buyer's solicitor on a variety of checks and paperwork.

In England, once both parties are happy to move forward, you will go through an "exchange," which is basically the point at which neither party can back out of the sale without incurring a very hefty penalty fee that would make it near impossible for the average person to pull out of the sale.

Oh, yes, you heard me right – you can pull out of the sale anytime up until the date of exchange with no penalty other than you don't get refunded for the payments you've already made for the house survey.

This makes buying a house in England a real on-the-edge-of-your-seat kind of situation where you're really not entirely sure for weeks on end that the house is actually yours.

The house Guy and I bought was on the market because the previous buyer literally pulled out on the day of exchange.

Assuming no one pulls out of the sale and the exchange goes ahead, you then will eventually "complete" on the sale, where all of the money gets transferred between parties.

Now, remember how I said there are no buyer's agents? If you're on the other end of the sale, buying the house, you have to undertake the process up until the offer completely on your own.

Instead of using your own estate agent to help you find properties, you have to find them on a few main listing websites and call the agency for each individual house to set up a viewing. After the viewing, if you want to make an offer, you will do this yourself directly to the agent that showed you the house or the agency they work for. The estate agent will then act as the go-between for the negotiations, but remember that they are essentially working for the seller.

There are also considerations in the UK regarding house buying like the "stamp duty," which is a tax. There are also different deals and schemes for first time buyers. It's also helpful to be familiar with your local area and the different problems that might come up when your solicitor undertakes the "searches" that show environmental, development and flooding concerns. Arm yourself with as much information as possible before embarking on the process.

Banking in the UK

While I warned you in the introduction that I wasn't going to tell you which bank to bank with (the rules and sign up requirements are changing all of the time), I do want to give you a quick run through of banking in the UK as an American expat.

The very first hurdle you'll come across is the struggle of opening a bank account when you first move here. Banks often want proof of address to open an account, which can be difficult if you haven't been in the UK a long time. Try to talk to banks before you move or look up their requirements to figure out how you can satisfy them as quickly as possible. Popular banks include: Halifax, Barclays, NatWest, Nationwide and HSBC.

The sooner you can get proof of address in the UK, the better.

If you're planning on ever moving back to the US, it would work in your benefit to keep your American bank account open. From cashing checks that your grandma gives you for your birthday to paying your student loans, American bank accounts come in handy even if you're living in the UK full-time.

While you shouldn't use an American card full time in the UK because of the fees from your American bank, you can use it to make purchases or take money out of ATMS while you get situated. Some American banks have relationships with banks in the UK that help bring down fees, so speak to them to see what your options are.

You can also sign up for a card like a prepaid Mastercard for travel or other travel-friendly credit card option that will allow you to deposit dollars into it and then convert it into pounds.

In terms of transferring money between UK and US banks once you get your new account set up, I use and would highly recommend an online service called Transferwise. If you do it through wire transfers, you will lose a lot of money due to exorbitant fees. I am in no way affiliated with Transferwise, but I love them because they cut out many of the fees and the money has always reached my account safely.

Within the UK, you'll find transferring money between bank accounts and making payments much easier in the US. Each UK bank account, no matter which bank you're with, has a "sort code" and "account number." To transfer money to another UK bank account, say to pay your friend back for the movie theater ticket they bought for you, you just need to know their sort code and account number and you can transfer the money for no fee just by logging into your online banking account.

Debit and credit cards in the UK are almost always just one step ahead of those in the US. They adopted the "chip and pin" system rather than the "swipe and sign" a lot earlier than the US, and nowadays almost all cards have the ability to do "contactless," which is paying by just tapping your card on the reader with no pin involved. Card readers here will still have the option to swipe your card and use chip and pin if you're trying to pay with an American card, but the contactless revolution is well and truly here.

If you are paying with an American card in the UK, it's best to try and go pay with an actual person rather than at a kiosk. I find that many kiosks and self-payment machines just aren't set up for international cards and it's a hassle to call the staff over to help you print and sign receipts.

Oh, and one more thing to remember: the vast majority of ATMS (called "cash points") in the UK do not charge a fee to withdraw money no matter who you bank with. As Americans, we're used to searching for our bank's ATMS to avoid fees, but you can pretty much stop by whichever ATM is closest to you in the UK and not worry.

Taxes in the UK

Taxes are basically the most boring thing on earth so I'm going to try and keep this brief because you should really consult a tax advisor on the matter, but you need to know a couple of thing about taxes in the UK.

Firstly, if you have a "normal" job in the UK and aren't self-employed, you don't need to worry about paying taxes as they're taken out of your paycheck each month and calculated automatically. What a system!

If you're self-employed in the UK, you do need to fill out your own self-employment tax forms.

Now, this comes as a surprise to many expats, but unless you have revoked your American citizenship (legally, not just in your heart), you have to also file taxes in the US even if you live abroad.

You often won't owe anything unless you make over $100,000 equivalent in the UK, as the countries have a treaty that tries to prevent double taxation, but even if you don't owe anything you still need to file.

The joys of filing taxes in two countries is one of those things that comes along with expat life and I can guarantee you that no one else likes doing it, so you just have to grin and bear it and spend a lot of time googling or speaking to an expert to figure out that year's tax requirements for expats.

In terms of sales tax, the rate is a standard 20% on most items and less or none if you're buying food, children's clothing, carseats, and more. This is built into the price of the item and not charged extra at the end.

Sending Mail

Within the UK, the mail system is run by Royal Mail and mail itself is usually referred to as "post."

Royal Mail are more or less efficient – it's of course a British tradition to complain about them, but I find that because mail has a shorter physical distance to go than in the US, my mail arrives a lot quicker. There are different kinds of stamps you can purchase depending on the type of letter size you're sending, but the main speed differences are "first class" and "second class." First class is supposed to get there the next day, while "second class" will go a bit slower and usually take a couple of days.

If you need something to arrive signed for or tracked, you can also purchase that service at a post office.

For American expats, the next obvious question is how you send mail between the UK and US– or, better yet, how your mom can send you that box of Cheez-Its you've been desperately craving even though you barely like Cheez-its when you're in the US and have no idea why you want them now.

Sending mail to the US isn't fast or cheap, but it can be reasonable for smaller items and weights. Letters are no problem – you just purchase international stamps from the post office that cost about £1 each. It's when you start sending packages that it can get pricey. Over the years, I've still found that the best way to send things to the US is via Royal Mail, rather than a service like FedEx.

You can also choose the speed you would like it to travel. One time, I wanted to send a letter to the US and I asked the woman if I could purchase the cheapest and slowest route. "Sure," she said. "But you should know that it won't get there for probably 60 days." "60 DAYS?!" I almost screamed. "How are they sending it, by boat?!" "Yes, actually," she replied.

I ended up going for the next option up, which was going to take about a week.

For people sending things from the US to you in the UK, the sticker shock is real. I used to get a lot of care packages from my mom and I would gasp at the upwards of $100 shipping charge I saw on the outside of the box. Needless to say, I get less of them now and instead I try to leave extra space in my luggage when I visit so I can bring back everything I need to.

Shopping in the UK

For the most part, shopping is an international language and it works the same in both countries – you pick something you want to buy, go up to the checkout, and purchase it.

There are some differences to keep in mind, though, starting with the fact that sales tax is included in the prices of items already. The price displayed is the price you pay. Guy gets so frustrated when he comes to the States because he forgets that we include sales tax at the end, so he always tries to get out the "perfect change" only to be foiled by the extra percentage.

Another big change happens at the end of your shopping experience at a supermarket, when you would usually expect an employee to bag your groceries and hand them to you. Not in the UK! You have to bag your own groceries while your cashier is throwing them down the conveyor belt at you, which is not a problem so much as a real shock for the first time you go grocery shopping in the UK and stand there like an idiot wondering who is going to come bag your groceries.

There is a small cost per plastic bag in the UK, which was done as an effort to try and get people to waste less bags and bring their own reusable ones instead. It seems to have done the trick as you can usually see Guy and I balancing 86 cans of beans and a banana on our head as we try to bring our groceries to the car after forgetting our reusable bags.

Online shopping is also popular in the UK, and you can order from places like Amazon UK (though you need to make a new account, it doesn't automatically switch over from your American one).

If you are going into a physical store, just make sure to plan you trip carefully as stores don't normally stay open as late as they do in the US, especially on Sundays when all of the major grocery stores around us close by about 4pm.

In terms of expense, you'll find that shopping for food is much cheaper than in America, while shopping for clothes is either comparable or a bit more expensive.

Clothing Sizes in the UK

When shopping for clothes and shoes, don't just automatically assume that your size in the US is the same in the UK. Shoes work on a completely different system, men's pants (trousers) are measured in centimeters rather than inches, and women's clothing runs on a smaller scale than in the US so a UK size 2 is a US size 6, and a UK size 10 is a US size 14 and so on.

The easiest way to avoid any pitfalls is to either keep trying things on in a store until you find what fits and note down your UK size, or look up a specific size conversion chart for that particular style of clothing and make an educated guess about your UK size.

American Stores in the UK

I've put together a list of some of the most asked-about American stores and their status in the UK, because I know that you don't want me to blather on about it and just want to find out if there's a Target.

Keep in mind that this is always changing, as chains open up and pull out of the UK, so even if there isn't your favorite store yet, there might be hope on the horizon.

Examples of American Chains that Are in the UK

McDonald's
Burger King
TGI Fridays
Dunkin Donuts
Chipotle
Five Guys
Baskin Robbins
Whole Foods
H & M
GAP
KFC
Starbucks

Examples of American Chains that Are Not in the UK

Target
Walmart
Sports Authority
Olive Garden
Outback Steakhouse

Bath and Body Works
Bed, Bath and Beyond
Wendy's
Chick-Fil-A
Any American bank
Any American grocery store (besides Whole Foods)
Kmart
Sephora
Liquor stores (alcohol is sold directly in grocery stores)

Phone Contracts in the UK

One of the biggest wins for American expats in the UK is the price of phone contracts here. I pay about £15 per month with a company called Three for unlimited data and more minutes and texts than I could ever use up. Brits are shocked by the sky high prices of American phone contracts, and those days are over for you!

If you're making a more short-term move to the UK, you may want to keep your American number active and simply pop out your American sim card and keep it in a safe place to then be able to use your American phone in the UK with a UK sim card. For expats, getting an international plan never makes sense as it's prohibitively expensive for the amount of time you will be abroad.

UK plans come as either a "Pay as you go" plan or a monthly installment plan. You'll get better deals on an installment plan, but you usually have to wait to get one of these until you have a bit of credit history in the UK or proof of address, so start with a "Pay as you go" plan if you need to.

To make calls back to the US, you can either burn up your minutes and data calling from your UK phone back to the US, or, better yet, use calling through an app like Whatsapp or others that allows you to call over WiFi.

Adaptors and Converters

There's no need to get rid of your electronics like phones, tablets, and laptops when coming to the UK (and you may not want to as keyboards are laid out slightly different in the UK so be aware of that if you purchase a computer here!) Instead, you'll just need an adaptor to be able to plug your US plug into a UK wall socket.

Most items are dual voltage nowadays, but if you do have a piece of equipment that can't handle the voltage: 230V (it will say somewhere on the product), then you also need what is called a "converter" which will make sure that your US item is equipped to handle the UK electricity strength.

It's Not Elementary

Parenting Kids in the UK as an American Expat

While being a parent in the UK hasn't been part of my expat journey yet (though I am a great babysitter), it's very common for Americans to come over with their children or to have kids while they are here.

If your family includes some little ones (or big little ones), I'd like to give you a starting point of what to think about in the UK when it comes to all things childhood.

Pregnancy in the UK

The number one thing that comes up when talking to Americans about their pregnancies in the UK is that the UK is much more hands off - in a positive way. This is an area where, on the whole, the NHS seems to shine.

The birth process on the NHS, which is the avenue most American expats use to give birth in the UK, is midwife-led and treats pregnancy holistically. It is seen as a natural part of life, rather than something that requires lots of hospital appointments and medical interventions.

Now, don't get me wrong - most people's experiences are that they are well looked after and if they sensed a problem during their pregnancy or weren't sure about a symptom, they could go in and get seen straight away.

Scans are typically done at around 14 weeks and at around 21 weeks. The first is to see how far along you are and the second to figure out the gender of the baby and check its anatomy. You will have more if you have a high risk pregnancy, but otherwise they won't keep scanning throughout the pregnancy.

Moms in the UK also felt that they didn't have their blood taken as much as in the UK during their pregnancies, which again is down to the more natural approach that your body will let you know if something is wrong, in which case they would investigate further.

There are also more organized groups in the UK for parents to meet other parents-to-be and learn about giving birth and parenting before the baby arrives. These are called "antenatal classes or "NCT" and can help you meet other pregnant women and get advice from caring professionals. While you can take courses during your pregnancy in America, expat moms found that the antenatal courses in the UK were much more helpful in fostering a community among parents and preparing you for birth and the parenting journey.

Giving Birth in the UK

When it comes to the end of pregnancy and finally bringing your new addition into the world rather than just letting it chill in your stomach watching Netflix, the UK continues its emphasis on birth as a natural human process.

That doesn't mean you have to give birth "naturally" with no pain killers, but it does mean that you will not automatically be encouraged to give birth in a sterile hospital room. If you have a low risk birth, you can choose between giving birth at home, giving birth in a midwifery birth center and giving birth in a hospital. Even in the hospital, the delivery process is led by a midwife with a doctor on call in case medical attention is needed.

You can also get pain relief on the NHS, including epidurals if you're in a hospital, but it is not the main method of pain management that they suggest. Instead, many women giving birth get what's called "gas and air" which is a pain relief method that you breathe in rather than being injected. There are also other injections and pain relief techniques that you can access during birth on the NHS, so don't worry if you're like, "give me all the drugs."

When you give birth, you will be in a private room just like you would be in the US, with your partner allowed to be in the room if you want them to be.

After You Give Birth

The differences in the US and UK after you give birth are more significant and probably noticeable than during the actual labor process, according to moms who have been there.

Firstly, unless you pay extra for a private room, you will usually be moved to a large, shared room or "ward" in the hospital with other moms and their newborns for recovery. There will be visiting hours, and many times your partner cannot stay overnight with you, which led many of the moms I talked to leaving the hospital earlier than they would in the US (the discussions around this pointed towards the fact that they perceived this as a good thing).

Once you and baby go home, you will have a health visitor in the UK come and see you at home to help you with the transition to parenthood and address any concerns. In the US, you usually need to bring your baby into the doctor's office yourself rather than having a home visit.

Later on, you will need to register the birth (the midwife or hospital you work with can instruct you on how to do this) and if you or your partner are a British citizen or have Indefinite Leave to Remain, your baby automatically becomes a British citizen as well!

And of course, perhaps the most important positive for moms giving birth in the UK is that unless you paid for a private hospital, you won't get a bill afterwards!

Schools in the UK

Whether your child has grown up in the UK or you have moved your children to the UK from America, you'll quickly learn the differences in the school systems across the pond. This is one of the major concerns that parents who are moving with children will go through, and for good reason - it can be an adjustment to figure out where your child fits in the system and how to make the transition as smooth as possible for them, particularly if they are in late middle school or high school.

The best way to get the full scoop on the options your child will have in the local area you're moving to in the UK is to actually get in touch with schools and people in your local area, but hopefully this rundown will help you wrap your mind around how the UK school system functions.

First, a child can go to "nursery" which is similar to the American preschool - a place to get acquainted with others their age and play and learn some basic things without it being actual "school." In England, the next step is "Reception," which is similar to the American Kindergarten. Children start reception usually in the school year in which they will turn 4.

From there, each level is referred to as "Year 1," "Year 2," etc up until "Year 12" being the final year, as opposed to the "First Grade, Second Grade, Third Grade" in the US. From Reception to Year 6 is called "primary school," equivalent to the American elementary school.

At the age of 11, students must take exams that will help determine which "secondary schools" they can attend. Secondary school goes from around Year 7 to Year 12, which puts the student at ages 11 to age 16. School is required for all students until the age of 16, at which point a student could choose to continue on towards the university track or go to a technical school or pursue a career.

Let's assume that your child will be continuing on in what an American would consider as "normal school." In Year 10 and 11, a student would take courses and exams called "GCSEs". This lasts for two years, and a student would take about nine of them between the two years. There are mandatory subjects, such as Math, English, and Science, but then a student can choose from other subjects like Drama, History, Religious Studies, Art, Computer Science, a Foreign Language and others. The subjects are chosen based on a student's interests and what they're thinking about doing at university (yes, the decision making starts early!)

After the two years of GSCEs, a student would be 16 and then embark on two years of "A Levels," that are essentially the equivalent to earning a high school diploma in the US. At this point, students have chosen what they want to focus on and take at least three or four A Level subjects.

They must then take the corresponding exam at the end of the year to earn the grade for that "A Level." I think of these similar to Americans taking AP classes, when offered - it is a comprehensive exam that covers a very specific subject.

At the age of 18, students then would move on to "university" if they go the higher education track. A "college" in the UK is a type of further education you would go to for a vocational course or possibly to study for your university entrance exams. What Americans think of as "college" is what Brits call "university." Americans might say, "Oh, I go to the University of Pittsburgh," but it would be equally true to say, "I go to college." In the UK, if you are in higher education and getting an undergraduate degree, no matter where you go, you are in "university."

When you apply to university as a British student, you also declare, from your application, what degree you want to do. Unlike the American system where you go to college and then can usually spend a year or so figuring out what you want to major in, British students will spend all of their university years (three in total) taking classes related to their degree.

This is, of course, a very basic look at the UK school system. Just like in the US where we have some K through 12 schools, some Elementary/Middle/High School systems and some in between, the local area and specific country in the UK will determine what kind of education system is available to your child.

The real challenge for many American kids in the UK, to be honest, is trying to figure out what they're saying with the blended British and American accent they pick up!

School Holidays

I can never keep track of when kids are out of school in the UK because it seems like they jump in and out constantly, but the real reason it feels like this is because many countries in the UK have shorter summers than the US and more breaks throughout the school year.

For example, English students will have about six weeks of summer from mid-July to the beginning of September, then a week off in October, then two weeks off at Christmas, then a week off in February, then two weeks off around Easter, then a week off in May.

Compare this to the US, where you will usually have a two month or longer summer, a week off for Fall Break, a week off for Spring Break, and a couple weeks off at Christmas. It's not that the UK students are out of school more total time throughout the year, it's just spread out much more.

Oh, and they don't call it "Easter break" or "Spring break," they refer to it as "half-term" or "school holidays."

The other important thing to know, both for your budgeting and for your sanity, is that you can be fined in the UK for taking your child out of school during "term time" without the school's permission. Not all areas will enforce it, but many Americans are shocked when they get a bill for the children's absence after their week off at Disney World that they didn't clear with anyone.

And even if you do request it, the school does not have to approve the child being away, in which case you would still have the pay the fine if you determined that you were still taking your child out anyway.

The Guilt Will Always Follow You
Coping with Guilt and Grief as an Expat

When I first wrote this draft, I was reeling over the fact that my grandma had just been diagnosed with small cell lung cancer. I was angry, I was upset, and most of all, I was guilty.

It was enough to have to deal with choosing a country for my wedding, but now I was struck with the injustice of not being able to be with my family in the harsher moments of life.

My husband suggested seeing if my job would let me work from there for awhile, but that wasn't enough. I didn't want to just go back for a couple of weeks – I wanted to be able to go to her house whenever I want, or at the very least fly to my hometown for a weekend.

People often tried to comfort me with things like, "don't worry! It would be like this if you lived in America too – you might not live near your family."

All I wanted to do was shake them and scream about how it's not the same.

Hopping on a 10 hour international flight is not the same as being able to casually take a Southwest flight home for the weekend. Can't you see that? Being separated by the Atlantic Ocean is not comparable to being separated by a few States or even an entire country.

In some ways, this is the scenario I had always worried about and the one that makes me the most resentful of my life here. I felt disconnected, despite my dad's best intentions to keep me in the loop with text messages. I felt alone, like I was watching my family try and tackle a beast while I sat on the sidelines and watched.

I wish that I could tell you, fellow expat or expat-to-be, that I knew of ways to deal with this pain, but I think it would be extremely delusional to sit here and give you advice about "skyping often" or keeping up with your family with letters and text messages. It would be pointless to pretend that the grief of living so far away could be fixed with a couple more trips home per year or a nightly Skype call.

The only thing I can say that means anything at all is that with every decision, there are pros and cons. If you had chosen to not become an expat, you would have missed out on all of the life shaping experiences of living in a foreign country.

Embrace the boldness that took you to a new country in the first place and use it to walk through the grief of living far away head on.

My grandmother passed away when I was coincidentally home for the holidays. I flew in on December 12th, saw her on December 14th, and she was incoherent soon after. She died on Christmas Eve, and I was left with the most painful guilt that came along with the years of her life and our in-person relationship that I have missed since I moved to the UK.

I carry that guilt with me today. I will carry that guilt with me tomorrow. I will carry that guilt with me for the rest of my life.

But I do know that she loved me and wanted me to be happy and live my own life, and if living in the UK was that for me, then she was supportive all the way.

If you find yourself struggling with this particular scenario of a loved one passing during your time abroad, know that you are not alone.

The Guilt of Living So Far Away

As I touched on in the story of my grandmother's death, there is a feeling that almost all expats will be faced with at some point or another: unending, nagging guilt.

There are two main types of guilt I can pinpoint, one being the guilt thrust upon you by other people, and the other being the guilt that you picked up on your own the day you decided to move to the UK.

Now, the guilt given to you by other people is the annoying type of guilt. It's what you would think of as an old fashioned "guilt trip," and it usually involves relatives or friends either being purposefully or accidentally passive aggressive.

This kind of guilt crops up when you send your sister a text on your four year old niece's birthday and tell her to wish little Suzie a happy day, and the reply you get back is something like, "I will! She would love if you were here in person to say it though, haha!"

Inevitably there will be some kind of emoji afterwards, letting you know that your sister does not really mean "haha," but more like "how dare you abandon the family this way, you absolute scum of the Earth."

Or something like that.

Parents are also great for the guilt, no matter how old you are or how long you've been an expat.

They don't mean to do it (well, some do, but we're going to give them the benefit of the doubt here). They just love you and miss you, and it's natural for them to express how much they miss you or wish you could be there on main holidays like Thanksgiving and arbitrary holidays like Arbor Day and random Tuesdays.

Friends are another excellent source of expat guilt, though it comes in different forms and mostly disappointment rather than passive aggressiveness.

Instead of "wish you were here!" it becomes a neverending stream of "it's okay, I understand why you can't make it to my wedding" and "hopefully we can plan a trip soon where we can all get together."

The external guilt doesn't stop when you go visit, either! You think, "okay, great, I have two weeks with my family, I'll make sure to please everyone!" and then you leave at the end of the two weeks exhausted from making so many home visits, annoyed that you didn't get to spend any time doing anything else besides going house to house like Santa Claus, and stressed out that Grandma Clarence is upset she only got to see you four times when Grandma Dottie got to see you five.

I'll reveal a little secret to you now: you could go live back in your hometown for two weeks, two months, two years – the rest of your life, and somehow that external guilt won't stop being piled on.

I'll also reveal something else that I think it's important for us expats to remember as we walk this crazy journey. Your friends and family heap this crushing sense of guilt onto you because they love you. Because it hurts your mom to know you live an ocean away, because your best friend misses you being there and going out for lunch and being able to support her from two feet away rather than 4,000 miles.

For the most part, people don't have malicious intent. They just love you. So when you're feeling stressed because Aunt Melinda is throwing shade on your Facebook page because you can't make it to your cousin Lily's wedding this year because you've got no time off and no money to fly home for two days, just try to love her instead.

If only our friends and families knew how much we beat ourselves up with guilt at times, they would probably back the heck right off.

Speaking of that guilt, we're now on to the second type – the self-inflected type that may make you wake up many nights in a cold sweat because you feel like the most terrible monster for leaving so many people and places you loved behind.

Aside from making friends and culture shock, this type of guilt is one of the hardest things for expats to come to terms with. It is insidious, burrowing into us in ways we don't even realize until something tragic happens and we're left on the other side of the pond, unable to make it back in time. It pops out at us when we Skype our parents and realize how much older than seem than when we last saw them, it creeps up on us when our nieces and nephews turn another year older and we start to wonder if they even remember who we are.

For me, this guilt manifests in a kind of constant internal battle of whether "it's worth it." I feel like I'm on a giant scale, with what I have in the UK on one side and what I could have had in the US on another. If I am going to choose to live so far away from what I knew, then I have to make sure it's worth it.

And when something happens that makes me feel unhappy in my life in the UK, I can't help but feel like I'm standing at the bottom of this weighed-down scale, looking up at US-me and thinking "it's not worth it." It's not worth it to live so far away from my best friend, it's not worth it to miss so many hours and days and months of my parent's lives, it's just not worth it.

And then I feel even more depressed at the thought that I made this giant life decision and yet I can't even make it worth the pain. And so on and so forth until you're a giant mess and sobbing in a ball in the corner and crying on your way past a field of cows and telling your boss that you need a mental health day because living in another country is just TOO HARD and you feel so, so guilty for all the people you've left behind. Or so I've heard.

What I have to say is this, and I repeat this to myself as often as I would repeat it to anyone else because it's easy to forget:

You have done nothing wrong.

It is likely that you live in the UK either because it was the best thing for you or it was the best thing for someone you love. You do not live here for "no reason." You are not maliciously out there in the world trying to stomp on other people's feelings. When your mom's birthday rolls around, you do not wake up in the morning going, "WOW! I'M SO GLAD I GET TO MISS THIS! (and if you do, then this section doesn't apply to you, so carry on please).

Experiencing other parts of the world and living in a different country is not a sin, it is not something to be guilty about, and it is not a reason to beat yourself up.

The guilt is normal – so, so normal. And sure, a bit of it is healthy to make sure you're keeping in touch and really making the most out of your life in the UK (except when, like me, you spectacularly fall apart as you'll read about in the next section and that's okay too).

But if you feel bogged down by guilt, whether it's thrust upon you by others or you picked out your own personal brand, try to release it a little bit at a time as you realize that experiencing your own life and following your passions and exploring the world on your terms is not now, nor has it ever been, wrong.

When my grandma died, I thought about how horrible I felt that I missed so many moments in her life in recent years and how I would never be able to get them back.

And then I thought of a world where I stayed put and visited her every day, despite my wishes to go abroad and my curiosity of what else was out there besides my hometown.

For me to think for a second that she was the kind of person who would have wanted that – who would have ever asked me, seriously, to give up on my dreams or not live the life I wanted – would have been so wholly incorrect and would have ignored the loving and caring person that she was.

The people in your life that you value just want the best for you. Sometimes, that goes against what's best for them, in that moment, but give them some credit.

We're all a little bit guilty at times, and the best thing we can do is be honest with each other while knowing that we, as the expats, are making decisions that we think are right for us, and our loved ones and friends back in the States ultimately want what is right for us, as well, even if it's painful.

It's Normal to Be Homesick
(Like, Really, Really Homesick)

"I need to get out of here," I wailed, frantically typing in "flights to Orlando" as I sat on my bed and cried.

My husband stared at me, not really sure what to do or how to help. I continued on, mostly because I was absolutely distraught and partially because nothing cures homesickness like dramatic declarations.

"I can't do this anymore. I need to go home." The more I talked, the more desperate I became. At points, I wanted to throw my laptop across the room and smash it into a million pieces because for some odd reason it was impossible to find a flight to America last minute for a discounted price. Can you believe it?!

It was October of 2017 and I was done. And I mean done. Done being an expat, done living in the UK, done commuting into London every day.

This wasn't a moment of homesickness, but instead a full on freak out brought about by years of dealing with visas and salary requirements, years of feeling like I didn't belong, years of being resentful that the UK doesn't stock

Pillsbury products – I mean, WHAT THE HECK.

The more flights came up, the more the idea became real to me. I could just buy a ticket, step on a plane tomorrow, and be back in Orlando. I could erase all of this, like it never happened, and just go home.

Erasing my life in the UK was something I fantasized about when things got hard – wouldn't it be easier to just hit the "destruct" button than to actually have to deal with my complicated emotions? A lot of times, it feels like that.

Of course, now, writing this out, it seems like I am the most monstrous person to ever consider such a thing, even if in a temporary moment of insanity. Erase my life in the UK? Forget about ever meeting my husband?

Yeah, it sounds horrible. It was horrible. But I also felt horrible. Some of the words I would have used to describe how I was feeling include: trapped, resentful, angry, annoyed, sad, heartbroken, mad, and did I mention angry?

At this point you're probably like, "girl, you need some therapy" and yes, that is very true, but I don't have time in my schedule for therapy right now so I'm writing this book. So there.

Honestly, I have had more than one of these freak outs where everything sucks and I just want to crawl into a hole that conveniently pops out back in America and then close the hole up behind me so all of the frustrations of the UK can't hurt me anymore.

Now, I wish I could say that I got over this moment and closed the flight booking window and went back to my blissful life in the English countryside, but what actually happened was I went through with booking the very expensive flight, got dropped off at the airport the next day by my husband, and went to America for a week.

I also wish I could say that while I was in America, I got some perspective on things and missed my life in the UK.

That did not happen.

Instead, I had the most blissful week in America seeing my best friend and my parents and my old life, and while it was a temporary quick fix, I wasn't ready to go back. It did, however, help serve as a reminder that America was only ever just a plane ride away and I wasn't actually in a prison however much I felt like it.

To date, that was the most dramatic moment of homesickness that I've ever felt, though there have been plenty of other moments (at least once a week, if not once a day depending on what I'm up to) where I long for the blue skies and open roads of Florida.

But that was the most – the crème of the crop – the "oh my God, is she actually going to pull through this one without leaving for America and never coming back." At no point before or after that have I fallen apart so spectacularly, but I'm starting to understand that all of these feelings of anger and resentment and frustration had been boiling for five years and it was finally ready for them to come out, much like how the pasta water boils over basically every time I cook because I turn it on high and then walk away while it erupts behind me.

As I've mentioned, I don't have all the answers. If I did, I would have probably been like, "Oh darling, I'm feeling terribly homesick today. Let me just talk this through and work this out and oh – no worries now, I feel better."

Instead, I rampaged through the house and wanted to break things and then angry-booked a ticket out of there.

So in lieu of providing you all of the answers, I want to tell you what I was angry about. Because maybe you're angry about it too. Or maybe you don't think you're angry about it, but you are. Or maybe you're still hardcore judging me and are like, "wow, girl can't adjust to the UK after five years, LAME." Or whatever.

Feeling Trapped

Firstly and probably most importantly, I was angry because I felt like an animal trapped in a cage. And not a cute fluffy Cockapoo or something. Like a really ugly Komodo dragon that its keeper kept locked away except for twice a year when it could come out for food and then it was hurried back into its cage again.

Anyway, so I was feeling trapped. For two reasons. One being that because of my visa requirements and my husband's line of work, we rely on my job to give us the steady income to meet the salary requirements. Having a full time job means that no matter how absolutely amazing your boss is about letting you take even more time off than you should be, you still can't choose to just go to America on a whim when you're feeling homesick without approval.

Of course, the whole issue is compounded by the fact that the reason you need the visa is to be able to live in the UK, and in a moment where you are desperately not wanting to live in the UK, it all seems futile and pointless and like you're following the rules of UKVI in order to get a reward that, in that moment, you don't want anyway.

No one said expat life was going to make sense, but I didn't anticipate it being this full of emotional land mines.

The other reason I was feeling trapped was because I had crashed my car a couple of years prior and since then, had been relying on my husband if I needed to go somewhere where I needed to drive. I felt physically trapped, bound to the house, despite good public transportation and my own two feet being able to get me to the grocery store nearest our house and our local train station.

(This is why I think learning to drive is a really necessary skill for any American expat in the UK, even if you're scared!)

Culture Shock

Often, we think of culture shock as something that happens when you go to a wildly different culture and experience it for the first time. It seems like both a reaction to something "extreme" and something that happens right away – an initial shock.

It's important to know that neither of these things are true. Culture shock can happen in any culture that is not like the one you are accustomed too, and it's not necessarily something that just goes away.

Many American expats don't really prepare themselves enough for culture shock in the UK, because you think – it's basically the same culture with a different accent and some tea and pubs thrown in! What could be so different?

Well, my friends! You would be wrong! British culture is very much its own entity, relatively unrelated to American culture despite sharing a somewhat common language. From the way people interact to the different systems in healthcare, schools and government, to the tiny differences like how the British "first floor" is the American "second floor" – it can be constantly mentally exhausting to adjust to life in the UK.

There are multiple stages of culture shock, as well, with the emotions you feel ranging from elation and amazement when you first arrive to the irritation and anxiety that comes with feeling like you're constantly battling against cultural differences and having to think much harder than necessary to complete even the slightest of tasks.

It's said that the final stage of culture shock is adaptation – you feel confident and comfortable in your new culture. But I would argue that in my experience and many others, culture shock can still go in cycles and symptoms of culture shock can still hit years or even decades after you make the initial move to the UK.

Especially if you are a newer expat, expect to feel these feelings. You may be confused, you may be anxious, you may be sad, you may be annoyed, and none of it may be your fault because you're just going through the symptoms of culture shock that everyone goes through when moving to a new place!

Losing Myself

Over the years, I've found that one of the inciting incidents of a bout of sadness, homesickness or full on depression comes with having lost yourself and who you are. It is very, very easy to do when you're trying to fit in to things happening around you and you have become the "token American" in a group of people.

You begin to become a caricature of yourself and how you present yourself to the world, and suddenly your entire identity is wrapped up in being an expat rather than the characteristics that defined your personality back in the States.

This, for me, happens when I forget what it is I used to love to do. Whether it's your favorite television show that you stopped watching because it's hard to figure out how to watch it from the UK or your favorite food that is no longer easy to find, it's easy to get so caught up in expat life that you stop doing these things or seeking out hobbies and other interests that used to make you happy.

For instance, one of my favorite television shows has always been *Gilmore Girls*. I've watched every episode multiple times, have all the box sets, and could quote endless lines of dialogue to you. It was my "comfort television" that made me feel safe and happy and less stressed.

But when I moved to the UK, the box sets didn't come with me because they were US region and wouldn't work in the UK. And the television I did watch was either British or something that my husband and I had decided to watch together. In between being a study abroad student or doing my Master's degree or then commuting every day into London for my job, I no longer carved out time to watch something that used to make me really happy.

Sometimes, this is natural. Our interests change and we move on from them. But last year, when I found that *Gilmore Girls* was available on Netflix in the UK, I watched some on a whim while scrolling through the options – and suddenly, I found a little piece of myself again. That person that I was in the US was coming back, bit by bit, if only I gave her the time and space to do so.

Now, I make sure to carve out time for myself and do what I want to do – the things that I am interested in. Even if it's something as trivial as carving out a Friday night to just veg on the couch and watch *Gilmore Girls* by myself, I feel like I am taking some control back of my life and reconnecting with my interests.

Thinking the Grass Was Greener

Sometimes, the wailing and gnashing of teeth that happens when you're so homesick happens because we have the idea that the grass is greener across the pond. When we're faced with challenges or even just minute things that get in our way, it can be easy to picture America as this ideal land where the sun always shines, we always get along with our friends and family and things just go more smoothly.

The problem with this attitude is that it's easy to idealize America or your hometown or whichever town you left and forget about the things that you didn't like there. When you're tired of fighting the NHS to get the prescription you want, you forget that it would have cost you thousands of dollars in America and only £9 in the UK. When you find it hard to make friends with the parents at your kid's school, it can be easy to put your child's old school on a pedestal despite the never-ending drama you dealt with there as well.

Often, I fall into the trap of associating America with my childhood and picturing that as the "alternative" to living in the UK. But if I were to move back to the US, I wouldn't just be spending my time driving around town aimlessly with my best friend and playing street hockey outside my house with the neighbourhood boys. I would have the same responsibilities and adult issues that I have in the UK, just in a different country.

Seasonal Affective Disorder

One thing to keep in mind if you've come from a sunny state like Florida or California is to appreciate that some of the mental strife you feel might come down to the weather and not necessarily just expat life!

Seasonal Affective Disorder, or SAD, is a type of depression that can be mild or severe that affects people usually in the winter months when the skies are grey, the sun sets really early, and the rain and cold can seem oppressive.

You can of course be used to these conditions and still deal with SAD, but if you're from a sunny climate and have never been faced with weather similar to a UK winter before, it can be a serious shock!

I tend to suffer with SAD from about November until March or April, with January and February being particularly bleak months in the UK.

I remember one birthday (February 12th) where I was struggling so much that I literally just lay in my bed and didn't want to get out to go do anything with Guy. He had to drag me out to take me to breakfast to try and cheer me up, and then as soon as we got home I climbed right back in bed and just stared at the ceiling until I fell asleep.

Keep track of your emotions in different seasons in the UK, and if you do find yourself feeling a bit of nothingness around the winter, make sure to try and stay as active as possible, get yourself a SAD lamp for some sunshine, and remember that this too shall pass – the sun can't stay hidden forever!

How Expat Homesickness Can Show Itself

For me, my homesickness tends to build up and build up while I suppress it down, and then eventually it will end in a dramatic display of waterworks and yelling at the top of my lungs that I hate everything about my life in the UK, even if it's not necessarily true.

It also, as I mentioned previously, comes out in the form of a mild or severe depression that lasts for days, weeks, or a couple of months at a time. When I found myself lying in bed for most of February one year, that was definitely a combination of Seasonal Affective Disorder and expat depression.

We don't all feel expat depression or homesickness in the same way, but I wanted to share some other ways it's manifested in me so you can bring this to your British partner or coworkers and be like, "SEE, I'M NOT CRAZY. IT'S NOT JUST ME!"

For example, when I have a stressful situation such as trying to learn to drive in the UK or dealing with paperwork bureaucracy in the UK, I will get really irritable and blame all of my feelings on living abroad rather than the actual problem at hand.

Also, any time I get into a fight with my husband, it's made ten times worse because my homesickness makes me feel like if our relationship isn't perfect, then there's no point in being here just to struggle anyway (not appreciating, of course, that no relationship is perfect).

Sometimes I get so homesick that instead of reaching out to my friends and family back home, I cut them off even more and isolate myself to make myself feel even worse for no particular reason.

And of course, it's a constant fantasy in my mind, when things get hard, to just book the next flight to America and forever leave everything in the UK behind. I dream about reverting back to my old life, dropping everything and just starting (back) over. I think about this more often than I'd like to admit.

What Should You Do if You're Really Going Through It?

While I deal with a low-level of homesickness at all times and have gone through periods of more intense expat depression that can be solved with just some self-care techniques or letting time march on, I do want to stress that if you are feeling depressed in the sense that you can't function in your normal life or you are left with these feelings of anxiousness and helplessness for months on end – get thee to a counselor!

There are even American counselors in the UK who you can talk to if you just can't see yourself identifying with a Brit who maybe hasn't experienced the same expat feelings as you.

But whatever you do, do not suffer in silence. When I have a spectacular meltdown and my husband says, "why haven't you told me these things?" I say that I don't want to tell him because I don't want to bring him down all of the time or complain about how much I'm struggling. That only makes the problem worse and makes me resent the situation more than if I had just said, "Hey! I feel homesick today!" and got it out of my system.

Expat groups are amazing for this, especially expat Facebook groups. If you post any sort of problem or concern or just a rant about being homesick or not adjusting to England, you'll have tons of Americans supporting you and telling you their stories so you don't feel so alone.

And that's what I really want to get across, here. Whether your homesickness shows itself as irritability or depression or anxiety or resentment or anger or sadness, you are not alone. These feelings are okay, and normal, and sometimes they'll last longer than others, but you are not a monster or a failure at being an expat by admitting to feeling these things.

Sometimes, being an expat sucks. And it's hard. And sometimes, maybe, certain areas of your life WERE easier back in the US.

But you're here. Or you will be here. And as much as it might be fun to listen to my stories of panic-booking a $700 one way flight to America last-minute, I want to finish with the next few chapters telling you my story of hope and of how to get through when it seems impossible.

Home Isn't a Place
Figuring Out Where You Belong

There is an odd phenomenon that comes along with being an expat in the UK, and that is that you soon realize you belong to a special group of people who live on a spectrum of "belonging."

"Belonging," it turns out, is a pretty important piece of life that helps us figure out who we fit in with, how we identify ourselves, and gives some sort of framework to our daily lives. As much as we can spread inspirational quotes about getting rid of labels, there's no denying that labeling ourselves is sometimes a necessity.

Before I embarked on expat life, I knew exactly where I belonged in the sense that I could easily fit myself into cultures and countries.

I was born, raised, and lived in America, and so therefore, I was an American. I was a college student at the University of Pittsburgh, so therefore, I was a Pitt Panther and also felt obligated to go to football games because people from Pittsburgh LOVE their football – who knew?

I wore shorts everywhere I went because I was a Florida native. I loved when my friends cancelled plans on me because I was an introvert. You know the drill.

Living in the UK as an American suddenly thrust everything I knew about belonging into a weird mess of confusing questions and changing inflections. While my accent has never changed, my inflections can sound more British or American depending on who I'm talking to.

When I come back from a visit to the US, my coworkers think I sound like I'm from the South (and explaining that central Florida is not culturally the South is too much for me sometimes so I roll with it). My mom sometimes thinks I sound British and wonders why I say strange things like, "shall" and "bin it."

And while I still hold the American identity and know that I AM American by birth and by upbringing and by the "USA" in my passport, suddenly there is a real battle over where I belong.

In the UK, it can feel a bit like I'm going through the motions of British life without actually connecting to them or thinking about them.

Sure, I say "swede" instead of "rutabaga," "sort it out" instead of "figure it out" and "shop" instead of "store." I know the social cues like sitting and taking forever and a day to sit down and talk to people after we finish eating. I'm used to phrases like, "the M25 is backed up" and "did you listen to Radio 2 this morning?" and "did you watch Bake Off last night?"

But in many ways, no matter how hard I try, I will always be sort of just swimming along, hoping no one will notice that I don't actually connect in the depths of my soul with these things – I just understand them and I go along with that social contract.

And that's not to say that these things don't come easily to me. Over time, you find that you do usually easily slip into these norms and vocabulary and ways of thinking. But saying "rubbish" and learning not to make eye contact on the tube is not the same thing as being British. Even getting a British passport, for expats who reach that citizenship phase, does not necessarily equate itself to feeling British.

For me, it's always a bit like I'm playing British. And I can play it really well. But at the end of the day, when I'm curling up in bed dreaming about eating Cheez-Its, it's still very apparent that I'm just playing.

Now you could argue that this all makes sense. Unless you're a third culture kid who grew up in lots of different countries, there is, for many people, an undeniable sense that no matter how long you live in a foreign country, your home culture will always be your most innate one that you feel in the depths of your being (this is getting very dramatic, this business on belonging, but stick with me).

I thought this too, in the first couple of years. Every time I would go back to America to visit, I would instantly think, "I'm home! These are my people! Someone just asked me a random question in line at the grocery store – I FEEL ALIVE AGAIN!"

And then, slowly, thing started happening in America that I wasn't there for. Giant political movements. New presidents. Social movements. National disasters. And my memory of these days and these movements have less to do with my experience with them and more to do with what I read about them or saw posted on Facebook from my friends.

The things I was tuned into, of course, were things like Brexit, UK immigration fights and trying to actually figure out who British celebrities were instead of just saying, "Who?!" every time a co-worker informed me that someone in the news died.

Along with that, the more I get acclimated to the British way of doing things, the stranger it is when I go back to America and find myself in old situations with a new perspective. It can be easy to forget which words Americans use for certain objects or foods because you're so used to saying the British ones, and the American "way of life" can suddenly feel foreign.

The last time I was in America, my husband and I went into a store at Disney Springs, the shopping area of Disney World.

"Hey there!" a woman from the back shouted as she rushed up to us. "Can I help you guys find anything today?"

I stood there, frozen, and could only awkwardly mutter a "No thanks, we're good!" in return. She smiled and walked away, always making sure she had our eye on us in case we suddenly came up with a question we needed her to answer.

"We need to leave," I hush whispered to my husband. "Now!"

He looked at me, confused, but acquiesced and I pushed him out the door.

"What was that about?" he asked as we were back out in the fresh air.

"I've lived in the UK for so long I forgot what it was like when American store employees talk to you! It freaked me out!"

Choosing to Be More than an Expat

One of the biggest mistakes I've made since moving to the UK is wrapping up my entire identity in expat life.

It's so easy to do this when making friends or being in the local community, especially if you live somewhere other than a big city. You can instantly become "the American," and it's one of the easiest things to talk about to make small talk with people. You seamlessly learn to ask people, "oh, so have you been to the States?" and then they regal you with the time they went to a wedding in Colorado or a week in New York City when they were six.

For me, I assumed this role readily because it made it a lot easier to figure out how to connect with people. I was comfortable being the American and somehow assuming the responsibility for always giving the "American point of view." I liked that I had a role to place in any given social interaction.

The problem with this, however, is when it extends into your inner life. Soon, being "the American" turned into identifying myself by how well I was surviving life as an expat, and when a bout of homesickness struck, suddenly I couldn't see past it or compartmentalize it as one facet of my life.

Even now, as I write this book, I am in many ways carving out an identity for myself as just an expat. But you have to remember and remind yourself that you are not defined by your Americanness if you don't want to be and that you are much more than your expat life.

Dig into your hobbies, connect with people about things you're interested in rather than what accent you have, and embrace your expat struggles and triumphs as a part of your life rather than the whole thing.

When You Visit "Home" and It's Not the Same

There are two ways that people often talk about visiting America while expats in the UK. One is to say how much more homesick it made them, realizing how much fun they had in the States or being able to be around friends and family.

The other, which comes up a lot more often than you would suspect, is when an expat goes back to the States for a visit and has a sudden epiphany that it's not the same.

Maybe the political climate is different than when they first left, maybe they didn't feel as connected to their friends and family, or maybe they had remembered things as better than they were. Whatever the reason, it can be really jarring and contribute to the feelings of not belonging anywhere.

If you're going back to the States for a visit and are worried about what it might be like, here are some of my best tips from years and years of trying to figure this whole thing out. These do not necessarily apply if you are re-entering and going to live back in the States permanently, but more for those of you who are visiting over the holidays or just throughout the year, with plans to go back to the UK when your visit is over.

Make a Plan

If you haven't been living somewhere for a while, you lose track of what your life was like there and what you did day to day. And in many cases, what you did day to day included things like a job or school that you're no longer taking part in in that area.

Maybe you're staying with your parents and so despite being 33 years old you feel instantly 11 again, or you're staying with a friend and don't have your own space and are going crazy because their adorable Chihuahua (bless him) is nipping at your heels every two seconds.

Basically, you're going to be out of your element both task-wise and location-wise, probably, and the best way to combat that is to have at least a rough plan of what you're going to do.

Not only does this help try and fit everyone in so you can assuage that expat guilt a bit, but it also gives you something to look forward to and helps keep you on a schedule so you don't spend the whole time listlessly sitting in the backyard with no idea what to do with yourself.

If your plans change, that's no problem – the point isn't to stick to the plan, it's to make one.

Don't Expect it to Fix Everything

When I threw up my hands in October of 2017 and booked a flight to America in an attempt to fix my homesickness, it did work temporarily. But the long term problem of me feeling homesick in the UK and the underlying problems I had with my life and with myself were not able to be fixed with just a few trips to Target (and I spend enough time in the clearance section to know that if that were the case, it would have come true by now).

Don't go on your trip expecting just the simple act of being in America to solve all of your problems and fix your life. Sure, it might give you some perspective and a new way of looking at your problems, but it's not a cure-all. Don't put that pressure on your trip and you'll enjoy it much more.

Do Something New

I have this weird desire when I'm back in the States to do all of the same things I used to. I want to recreate my "old life" exactly, down to where I go out to eat, where I shop, the order I do things in, etc.

This can be fun for a couple of days, but you're not the "old you" anymore, and your interaction with your hometown or your family's town shouldn't be the exact same as it once was.

To try not to get so bogged down in reliving your past life, make it a point to do new things around town that you either haven't done before or that have opened up since you've moved away. Not only will this help give you a new perspective on the town, but it will give you more life experiences and that's what growing as a person is all about.

Appreciate it for What it Is

We can have this constant battle in our head of "which place is better" when we're living life as an expat. Just as the often repeated advice is to not compare the UK to America when you first move to the UK, the same goes for when you're visiting America. Some things will be better than the UK, and some will be worse, and that is the nature of life. But try to appreciate America and your hometown for what it is, rather than comparing it (even if the comparison would put your hometown ahead – it's not helpful if you are trying to succeed as an expat in the UK!)

This really just goes along with not putting pressure on the trip to be anything in particular and letting yourself enjoy your time there without it bringing out a whole host of emotions that aren't helpful.

Share Your Feelings with Other Expats

Did I mention it's common to have conflicting feelings when visiting the States are living in the UK? Like, really common. If you're having weird feelings about it, for whatever reason – maybe it wasn't what you thought it would be, or maybe you do think the grass actually is greener – talk to other expats about it! Trust me, they've felt it before or know someone who has!

Of course you can talk to your family and friends about it, but if they're not also expats it can be very difficult to empathize even if they can logically try and picture what you're going through. But other expats will be able to say "yep, I've felt that" and "oh, god, yes – SAME!" so you know that you're not alone in your feelings and can instead just let them go or sit with them rather than questioning every thought you have and what it means and if you're alone in it.

The True Definition of Home

I read a quote once that sums up exactly what I was feeling perfectly, from the book *The Girl Who Chased the Moon*. It very simply says, "I'm homesick all the time. I just don't know where home is."

The idea that "home" is one place is absurd, as many expats will tell you that both (or even more than two) countries truly feel like home. I often have to clarify for my husband "which" home I'm talking about, as I refer to both England and America as home equally.

It also defies reason that home even IS a place. It can be, but it can also be the people you surround yourself with. If all of the people you knew moved away from your hometown, you might still feel nostalgia for the times that you had there as you drive by, but would you really feel "at home" living there in a house surrounded by people who weren't there growing up?

If we can flex our idea of what "home" is, we can learn to better cope with the negative feelings that can creep into an expat's life.

Ultimately, I believe that you have to be at home within yourself. If you live your life authentically and fully and work on maintaining a high self-esteem and confidence in your abilities, you can feel at home no matter where you are in the world. The baggage that we create in our lives follows us everywhere – it does not diminish or get easier simply because we're in a new country or equally, when we've returned to our "old one."

As hard as it is for me to accept, if I really got to the bottom of things, I would say that the problems we have as expats are not often down to the place. They're down to us. In some ways, that's annoying and terrifying because it requires you to actually change your mindset and deal with things rather than wandering around complaining about how small your house is and how different the food tastes and how stupid your coworkers are.

In other ways, it's freeing. I don't mean to get all mushy and self-helpy because like, hello, have you read the part about me threatening my husband I was going to abandon him and move back to America in an instant? But honestly, I know that if you learn to love yourself, you will learn to love your life no matter where in the world you are.

It Can All Be Wonderful
The Upsides of Life in the UK

Despite the last couple of chapters that may have left you slightly down about the struggle of expat life, I wanted to end on a more positive note. For me, expat life in the UK has been an opportunity to really get to know myself and how resilient I can be. It hasn't all been butterflies landing on my head as I walk to work or billions of pounds in cash dropping down from the sky, but it has been the journey of a lifetime and an experience that, at the end of the day, I am grateful for (even when I'm rage smashing my head against the wall).

Why It's Cool to Live in the UK

If you're wondering about the practical benefits of living in the UK that I've found – maybe you're moving here soon or maybe you just need a reminder – here are some of my favorites.

Travel Made Easy

There is no getting around the fact that since living in the UK, I've been able to travel to Italy, France, Germany, Ireland, Spain, Austria, Norway, and Denmark. If I were still living in the States, there is no way I could have made that many trips, or if I did I'd have to force it all into one major trip where I spent one night in each place and remembered 0.5% of what I saw.

The UK is in such a fantastic location for travel that seeing more of the world is made possible here. I've been to Paris by train, France by car and Spain in a plane (yes, I just included that one because it rhymed). You've also got Iceland about a four hour plane ride away, Bermuda in between the US and the UK, the north of Africa very close by, some lovely islands dotted around, and the rest of Europe.

Not to mention that within the UK itself, you'll have three other countries to see other than the one you're living in. The mountains of Scotland look different to the coastline of Wales which differ from the gorgeous landscapes in Northern Ireland and the natural monuments in England.

The transportation infrastructure in the UK is also lightyears ahead of what I was used to in the suburbs of Florida. London is renowned for its transportation, with the tube winning tons of awards for being easy to navigate, and buses, trams, and trains are very popular in the rest of the UK. While there are some remote areas where you do need a car, it's very easy to live in an area - even a small village – that has public transportation to get you to where you want to go.

And when you want to go back to the States? Increasingly, flights are getting cheaper and cheaper across the Atlantic which means that you no longer need to spend thousands of dollars just to go back and forth.

History, Culture and Meaning

While I can't really remember what happened yesterday, the UK holds a treasure trove of history that dates back to over 800,000 years ago. I can't even comprehend that number, but there you have it!

The years, decades, and centuries of history in the UK is really impressive when you stop to think about it. And you don't even need to do much thinking, because you can go see this history for yourself during your time as an expat.

From the Roman Baths to Stonehenge to Westminster Abbey to the thatched roof cottages all over the place, the history and traditions of the UK run deep. You don't just get to learn about Shakespeare, you get to visit his grave. You don't just get to picture yourself as royalty, you can go visit Windsor Castle or Buckingham Palace in the summer to see how they live their public lives.

The town I used to live in in England, Great Missenden, was also the home to Roald Dahl for many years and he is buried in one of the churchyards there. To think that a literary figure so influential to me would have so much history in a village I regularly wandered the streets of was awe-inspiring and put into perspective how lucky I was to live in the UK.

The same goes for thinking about the culture and meaning behind what you encounter in the UK. Sure, there are more purpose built developments popping up as the years go by, but much of what is here has been here for hundreds, if not thousands of years. The lanes in the countryside are small not because the Brits wanted to be annoying about it, but because those lanes were developed for horses before the inventions of cars. When Parliament is in session, there are plenty of weird ways of doing things that don't make sense on first glance, but do when you discover that there is a tradition behind it.

Health Services

You could debate for days the pros and cons of a nationalized health service and a private one, but I will be the first to say that not having to worry about payment when I go to the doctor aside from a less than £10 prescription fee is incredible.

Calling an ambulance for a friend or relative and not needing to give them insurance information is so freeing.

Knowing that if you were to come down with a serious illness, you could focus on getting better rather than starting a GoFundMe is invaluable.

Parents who have children here being able to focus on their children's first few days of life rather than dealing with hospital bills is so comforting.

Beautiful Places to Go

I touched on it earlier, but the UK is truly made up of some drop dead gorgeous places, and just when you think you've seen it all, something will surprise you.

I had lived here for seven years, for instance, before ever seeing the amazing coastline of Cornwall. When my husband brought me there, to a place called Kynance Cove, I looked down to see beautifully turquoise water and a seal bobbing up and down while looking at me. I could have cried then and there over how beautiful it was, and I was so enchanted that he had to tear me away.

Explore the fells in the Lake District that stand so elegantly above the water. Discover hidden gardens in London where you can lose yourself for hours and feel like you're a million miles away from the city. Check out the jaw-dropping beauty of the Scottish isles with their sandy beaches and take a trip to Edinburgh to see the castle tower over the city. Go surfing on the coast of Wales, or just take a road trip through the Cotswolds to see miles of countryside that sparkles in the summer sun.

If you're into big cities, London is one of the best in the world, and if you want cottages on cobblestone roads, head to the Cotswolds. Liverpool is quirky with tons of Beatles history and an absolutely breathtaking cathedral, while Oxford will give you the Harry Potter vibe that you've been craving.

Why Being an Expat is Awesome

Adaptability Becomes Your Middle Name

It's easy to get stuck in a rut in our lives and think that we couldn't imagine how other people live differently than us. We get used to our giant fridges, our giant cars, our giant roads, and we don't even think for a second about what life might be like if we didn't have those luxuries.

And then, suddenly, you find yourself living in your home in the UK trying to create a makeshift air conditioner out of a piece of wood and someone blowing on a dandelion really fast.

Adaptability is one of the biggest keys to success and getting us to try things a bit differently and learn a "new normal." It gives us confidence in so many other areas of our lives as well.

On the same fateful trip where I panic booked a flight to America due to expat homesickness, I ended up in Bermuda.

Yes, you read that right. Bermuda. I had booked a direct ticket from London to Orlando, and I ended up being diverted to Bermuda due to a medical emergency on board.

This trip involved spending the night in a foreign country, being transported across an island in the middle of the Atlantic ocean at 11pm at night with a bunch of other strangers to my hotel room, having to navigate Bermudian immigration forms when I wasn't even planning on going to Bermuda in the first place, and many other very strange things that all seem very bizarre to me now.

A previous me would have crumpled at the thought of it all – I was on my own, and while I had the airline supporting me and putting me up, I still had to figure a lot of things out on my own.

Expat me just laughed at it all. Every single time the situation zigged, I could zag with it. The whole situation become comical, and something to laugh at as I confidently figured out what to do and who I needed to speak to.

Sure, maybe it's not the hardest thing in the world to adapt to spending an unplanned night in Bermuda of all places, but my expat experience had taught me how to turn a situation that I would have found scary into something I could handle with ease.

You Have No Choice but to Grow

The saying that "growth is just at the end of your comfort zone" is very true, and it's especially true for an expat who suddenly learns that almost nothing is in their comfort zone. Between figuring out how to work the dishwasher to wondering why people keep asking you if you're alright to debating whether or not you should offer a round of tea at work, expat life starts off uncomfortable.

I look at it like this: there are also some things in life that you have a choice about learning. I can choose to learn calculus (but I already did that and failed miserably). I can choose to open a book and read about lemurs. I can choose to exercise and learn about good diet.

But I don't *have* to do any of those things.

The beauty of being an expat is that much of the learning that is done is done because we must if we want to succeed. You have no choice but to get used to driving on the other side of the road if you want to be able to make it to the grocery store. You have to learn the British healthcare system if you want to get that lump checked out.

This can be terrifying and lead us to feeing trapped, like I talk about earlier in the book, but it's also amazing because we end up doing it, even if our inner selves are resisting every step of the way.

Being an expat comes with so many great things that happen because you have no other choice but to let them happen. It's sink or swim, and even if you're kicking and screaming your way down the river while wearing inflatable floaties, you're still going to get there in the end.

You'll Drink Resiliency for Breakfast

Similarly to how we have no choice but to grow, you learn a resiliency as an expat that you wouldn't develop had you stayed in familiar territory. Not only do we learn to push past our comfort zone, but we learn to pick ourselves up and push past it again when we fail or make mistakes.

Many of us don't come as expats with the choice to immediately turn around and go back to the States. You're in it for the long haul, and even if that long haul is just a couple of years, you know that you have to keep carrying on even when it's 8 different types of confusing trying to figure out how to sign your kid up for school or do your taxes from abroad.

I've lived in the UK for seven years with no intention of living full time in America anytime soon, and so that means that for as many times as I fail making friends here, I have to dust off my bruised ego, squash down those introverted tendencies, and keep. on. trucking.

Bouncing back from things you don't understand and things that don't go right becomes a part of your everyday life, and that's a super healthy thing to learn.

A Chance to Practice Gratitude

One of the proven ways to live a happier life is to focus on gratitude. It sounds hippy dippy, and sometimes when you're just at the end of your rope with life in the UK, it can be very easy to give up being grateful at all. But the point is that practicing being grateful is much more effective when you are going through the ups and downs, not just when you're living in a million dollar mansion in Connecticut with a butler and a unicorn shaped swimming pool (oh, wait, is that anyone else's dream or just me?).

Learning the art of practicing gratitude and finding some sort of good in your situation is a great life skill and one that all expats have to master at one point. Otherwise, you'll just become the person who complains about their life all of the time and yes, I have been that person, but it's not a great way to spend your days and also really doesn't help in your relationships with your partner, friends, or family.

Having the ability to grit your teeth through your homesickness and be grateful that at least the sun is shining for once in England or you have the day off tomorrow or you have two hands that function to help you bake a cake to drown your sorrows in – it's all helpful and a worthwhile thing to learn.

You Will Learn More About Yourself than Ever Before

To be an expat is to have your life altered in a huge way. For as many times as you could move across America, trying to find yourself, I truly believe that you will never learn more and never be pushed more than when you leave the home culture you grew up in.

When I first left for London, I was a timid, quiet person who hadn't yet found her voice. I didn't feel as if I had a lot to say, or that people would be interested in what I said even if I thought it worthy of saying.

I also dealt with social anxiety, hypochrondria, and other poor coping mechanisms for figuring out the world around me like comfort eating endless piles of pasta.

My expat journey was gradual – a study abroad semester, then a Master's, then a relationship and now a marriage and a job, but at every turn my core self has been shocked into learning something more and becoming something more.

I am still daily embracing the idea that I cannot run from my baggage and have to carry it around with me, wherever I am, but my expat life in the UK has pushed me so much further than I ever thought I could go.

I never dreamed I would feel so capable and so confident in writing even this book. Tens of thousands of words about my expertise and my thoughts and my experiences that I previously would have locked away.

I would and will never be a social butterfly, as my mom would call it, but I have been able to form and maintain relationships here that would have been so far out of my comfort zone back in the States, where I always had my best friend to lean on.

Even on days when it's difficult and I want nothing more than to curl up in a ball and cry myself to sleep over the injustice of not having instant access to Cheez-Its, I can acknowledge that who I am today is a direct result of being an expat and the things I have learned along the way.

Have Courage

Being an expat is a courageous, daunting thing. Whether you do it for love or for a job or because you have been swept away by the beauty of the UK, there is nothing easy about it for many of us. Like most things in life, if it were so easy to adjust and adapt and live your best life here, it wouldn't feel so rewarding when you finally do.

This is what I want you to take away from this whole, crazy book on all of the things Americans have to figure out in the UK. You took, or are taking the step to move abroad. That, in and of itself, showed that you have a desire inside you to push yourself and to experience the world in ways you haven't before.

On the good days, celebrate this. You are strong and brave and you are soaking in so many experiences that others can only dream of. You are powerful and adaptable and able to handle the roadblocks that life puts in your way. You have made tough choices and you have come out better for it.

And when the days are bad, remember this. You are strong and brave and you can put one foot in front of the other. You can pass that driving test, even if you failed eight times before. You can make a new friend in your gym class, you just need to keep trying. You will feel okay again, even if you find yourself in a pit of expat depression and just need some time to process it.

What you feel is normal. The confusion at why you're being offered "squash," the guilt of living so far away, the sheer delight when you get to plan a weekend trip to a gorgeous bucketlist destination or a British person approves of the cup of tea you made them. The desire to erase your UK life and go back to America, the sadness of seeing milestones pass by in your family back home while you're not there, the frustration of watching your

British partner leave soap all over the dishes.

If you're happy when you visit America, that's great. If you're sad when you go, it's okay too. If you've cried over vegetables or misunderstanding the customer service guy on the phone or just over your existence in the UK at the current moment, I have so been there.

It's all part of the process, all part of American life in the UK, and most importantly, you are not alone.

About the Author

Kalyn Franke is an American expat in the UK who came over as a student, fell in love, and decided to stay (despite promising her mom before she left that she absolutely would not marry a British boy). She and her husband, Guy, live in a small house outside of London because life is expensive and all of their extra money goes towards trips to Disney World and buying cookie cake from ASDA.

She is the owner and content creator behind GirlGoneLondon.com, a website that started as a hobby to talk about the craziness of expat life and eventually grew into a sizeable website with actual information and not just musings on Pop-Tarts. Though, she does really love Pop-Tarts (Brown Sugar Cinnamon and Chocolate Chip Cookie Dough, if you're wondering).

Made in the USA
Las Vegas, NV
21 July 2021